Lois Lowry

The Giver

Teacher's Guide

by Mechthild Hesse

Ernst Klett Sprachen
Stuttgart

Die Autorin dankt Britta Putjenter, Eugene, Oregon,
für Anregungen und für die sprachliche Durchsicht des Manuskripts.

Dieses Lehrerbuch bezieht sich auf die Textausgabe von *The Giver*, Klettbuch ISBN 987-3-12-578140-5.

Verweise auf die Textausgabe werden in Kurzform angegeben: **29** 18 = Seite 29, Zeile 18
Der vorliegende Teacher's Guide folgt den orthografischen Konventionen des amerikanischen Englisch.

Neue überarbeitete Auflage von ISBN 978-3-12-578141-2

Bildquellennachweis:

Cover Klett-Archiv (Hanjo Schmidt), Stuttgart; **Cover** Shutterstock (Alex Staroseltsev), New York; **51** Shutterstock (Katerina Davidenko), New York; **56** Anna Hesse (nach Bernhard Heisigs *Gewieher*); **91** Lois Lowry; **77 – 85** Shutterstock (Alex Staroseltsev), New York

1. Auflage 1 6 5 4 3 | 2019 18 17 16 15

www.klett-sprachen.de

Sprecherin: Astrid Proctor
Tonstudio: andreas nesic, custom music, Stuttgart
Recordings of first three chapters of *The Giver* (© 1993 by Lois Lowry) by kind permission of Harold Ober Associates Incorporated.

Autorin: Mechthild Hesse
Redaktion: Hartmut Selke, Debby Böhm

Layoutkonzeption: Elmar Feuerbach, Sandra Vrabec
Gestaltung und Satz: DOPPELPUNKT, Stuttgart
Umschlaggestaltung: Sandra Vrabec
Titelbild: Hanjo Schmidt, Stuttgart
Druck und Bindung: CEWE Stiftung & Co. KGaA, Germering
Printed in Germany

ISBN 978-3-12-578137-5

9 783125 781375

Contents

Abbreviations

S	students	sb	somebody
HW	homework	sth	something

Online Links

Throughout the Guide you will come across a number of online links / QR-Codes. You can either enter the Online Code in the search field of www.klett-sprachen.de or scan in the QR-Code. You will then be directed to additional material which you can download and use in class:

1. Audio files: The first three chapters of *The Giver* have been recorded, so your students can listen (or listen and read along) to them in class.
2. Additional texts: Text excerpts from adult dystopias along with discussion questions.
3. URLs: All the URLs mentioned in this guide are listed online, so you can access the relevant page by clicking on these links, rather than tediously copying them out. This is also where we will inform you of any changes to links.

i. Preface to the new Teacher's Guide

With this new Teacher's Guide teachers are given a choice: to either use the novel extensively or use just the film *The Giver* (released in 2014). The first part, "Teaching the novel" has remained largely the same as the original, now out of print version. However, the teaching unit has been changed at the end, where teachers can use the film for a critical comparison of novel and film. Also, the worksheets have been redesigned and have become more user-friendly (easier to copy and use in the classroom). They are now at the end of Chapter II *Teaching the novel.*

Since 1998 when the first Teacher's Guide came out, Lois Lowry has written three companions to the novel that now make up *The Giver Quartet*. Summaries of the three companions have been added to chapter IV as well as an excerpt from *Son*, which is the last novel and in some ways a conclusion. In *Son*, the fate of Gabe's birthmother, her longing for her son and Gabe's yearning for his mother are the main topics. People who have been asking Lois Lowry to tell them what *The Giver's* ending means finally get an answer to this question. Of course, *The Giver* can be read and understood without reading *Son*. The open ending leaves learners a lot to think and write about.

One focus of teaching the novel in class is writing. My teaching experience is that students are frequently required to produce various text forms in writing (especially in tests and written exams) but are rarely taught how to do so (cf. Hesse 2001).

Chapter III focuses only on teaching the film. This chapter was designed for teachers who do not want to spend so much time on teaching the novel, but want to confront learners with the futuristic concept and train viewing and listening comprehension, combined with speaking and writing skills. In this teaching unit the novel is only used at the very end. Teachers can of course also choose to use tasks and worksheets from the previous Chapter II.

The film has tried hard to do justice to the novel, but changes focus and also the plot to a certain extent. As Lois Lowry predicted in the interview in 1998 the film people needed action. And they got it by adding a love story, a bike chase at the end, the use of high tech technology and attractive landscapes. This and the selection of star actors make the film a real Hollywood movie. Hollywood movies are all about spending and making money in order to attract viewers. It seems to me that by using these "ingredients", young people are attracted as the desired target audience.

What is good about the movie is that it focuses on Jonas' dilemma that Lois Lowry created: the moral decision to save a baby, to reach Elsewhere and to bring the memories back to the Community. The close relationship to the Giver is well depicted. Jeff Bridges (the Giver) is not only a wise old man, but he is also like a "buddy", a friend for Jonas. The Chief Elder (Meryl Streep) has been given a more prominent position and appears several times throughout the story, but as the visual representative of the government her frequent appearances seem necessary.

All in all I think that, in spite of the numerous negative film reviews, the film can well be used in the EFL classroom. Students who have both read the novel and watched the film could be asked to compare novel and film and write their own review and/or discuss their views in class.

ii. Preface: A student-centered approach to the novel

The Giver is an extraordinary novel and it is exceptionally well suited to English language teaching. Given the point-of-view chosen by the author, the events in the novel and the information about the Community that the young protagonist lives in are revealed slowly, bit by bit to the reader. This makes for suspenseful reading.

In addition, the questions raised in the novel are universal. The idea of a future society in which problems have been overcome, in which people behave politely towards each other, in which no wars exist, is of great interest to young people. The idea of *so-called* feelings contrasted with *real* feelings makes young people reflect on the genuineness of feelings in general. And then there is the matter of death and of saving other people by bearing some of their burden that is central to the Judeo-Christian tradition. And above all, there is the theme of memories, which help people overcome loss and also make them part of history. You may well choose to read and discuss *The Giver* with your class chapter by chapter from beginning to end.

The topics raised by the novel will guarantee lively discussions in the classroom. The procedure suggested in Chapter II of this Teacher's Guide, however, is different. I would like to suggest that you be more open in your assignments, that you guide at the beginning and have your students research certain topics while they are reading. They will thus become the experts on the topics they have chosen. This approach makes both the students and the teacher the learning center: both learn from each other, listen to each other's insights and try to find out more about the book by using additional materials from different media.

After the first three chapters of joint reading and a carefully planned session on how to proceed, students have to read the book by themselves, but each one of them has a task to focus on, which makes him/her an expert on a theme in class presentations, discussions and writings. In addition, the students are encouraged to accompany their reading by keeping a reading journal or by transforming key passages into a radio play or film script.

A further goal pursued here is expanding the students' writing capacities. This of course has to be preceded by thoroughly planned class communication activities and discussions that are supposed to prepare students for writing assignments, which ultimately may help them improve their command of written English. In this process there is to be a progression from personal, spontaneous responses (reading journal) to text-based responses, and ultimately to consciously planned texts, which are rooted in students' interaction with the text and with other readers (classmates, teacher, other readers in the world). This process is meant to improve our students' ability to think and to express themselves orally and in writing.

I The novel

1. Structure and summary

The novel can be divided into three major parts:

Chapters 1–8	Exposition: the reader is introduced to the main characters and to some aspects of life in Jonas' Community. The reader learns that the "Ceremony of Twelve" is a very special event: at this ceremony each 12-year-old is assigned a lifetime job by a central committee and thus enters adulthood. Jonas is very apprehensive about the coming Ceremony of Twelve. Chapter 8 is the first climax of the story in which Jonas is not assigned a job, but is selected to become the Receiver of Memory.
Chapters 9–18	All the memories of the world as they existed before the present society, which is devoted to the principle of "Sameness," are transmitted to Jonas by the former Receiver (and now The Giver). Jonas thus learns about things that no longer exist in his Community, like color, weather, and love, but also about war and hunger.
Chapters 19–23	Realizing that "release" is a euphemism for killing, Jonas understands that the stability of his Community is bought at a high price, namely the killing of certain unwanted people, e.g. the weaker child when twins are born, babies who need more care than others, misfits and the old. With the Giver himself, who is becoming increasingly critical of and bitter about this society, he makes plans to escape (Chapter 19 is the second climax in the novel). When Gabriel, a "newchild," is threatened with release, Jonas is forced to flee without the Giver's help. The ending of the book is open: it is uncertain whether Jonas does in fact reach "Elsewhere," where he hopes to find freedom of choice and true feelings.

2. Overview of chapters

Chapter	Content	Observations
1	Jonas is frightened by a low-flying aircraft and feels apprehensive about the upcoming December ceremony.	"Release" mentioned for the first time: pilot who made the mistake of flying too low over the Community will be "released". Family goes through ritual of "the telling of feelings," which seems to be a form of social engineering. Mother talks about a rule which demands that repeat offenders must be released.
2	In a talk with Jonas his parents attempt to relieve him of the fear he feels about the coming Ceremony, during which the 12-year-olds receive their lifetime assignments.	Hierarchy is explained: committee of Elders and Receiver decide about rules to be adhered to by the rest of the Community.
3	Jonas' father brings Gabriel, a newchild, home for extra care. Jonas remembers a humiliating experience when he was reprimanded through a loudspeaker for taking food (an apple) away from the recreation area. He had done this to find out more about the apple, which seemed to have changed in size and shape.	Jonas, with his pale eyes, is different from other citizens. Gabriel, the newchild, also has light-colored eyes. Assignments have different social values (e.g. birthmother is not an honored assignment).
4	Jonas does his volunteer hours at the House of the Old where he bathes Larissa, who tells him about a release ceremony.	More regulations and methods of social engineering are mentioned. The exact release ritual for the Old is described.
5	In the dream-telling ritual Jonas tells his family about his first "Stirrings": he dreamt at night that he wanted to bathe Fiona, a good friend. His mother tells him that he will have to take medicine against the Stirrings from now on.	Another way in which people are manipulated and conditioned is by the compulsory dream-telling ritual, in which everybody has to recount their dreams. Sexual impulses must be curbed through treatment (pills).
6	The days of ceremonies bring big changes for children growing up. Jonas becomes increasingly nervous before the second day of the ceremonies when the new Twelves receive their assignments.	More rules and regulations are explained. Rumors about reactions of people not satisfied with their assignments are reported. Dissatisfied citizens can apply for Elsewhere and be released. Jonas believes in the wisdom of the committee's decisions, which are based on careful observation.
7	All the Twelves receive their assignments but Jonas is skipped. He is very shocked and tries to work out what he has done wrong.	Further values of the Community: "precision of language" (**48** 31) – lack of such precision is severely punished, as Asher's example shows – and curbing of impulses "that might set you apart from the group" (**46** 15).

Chapter	Content	Observations
8	Jonas is selected as the new Receiver of Memory, a singular, most honored position in the Community. It requires training and certain qualities that the Committee is certain Jonas has. He is very unsure of himself but by observing certain changes in the audience, comes to believe that he does indeed have the "Capacity to See Beyond" (**54** 15).	The pale eyes of the old Receiver are mentioned. He has a prominent position but obviously is not well-known as he does not speak in public. The Chief Elder concedes that a previous selection 10 years ago failed.
9	Jonas prepares himself for his training by reading the rules he has to follow. They seem to be different from everyone else's, which is very unnerving to him.	Additional information on the previous selection of a Receiver is given in a secretive way. Rule 8, "You may lie" is most confusing to him. He wonders if other people have received the same rule.
10	On his first day of training Jonas is stunned by the large number of books and the unusual furniture in the old Receiver's room. His job has exhausted the old Receiver; he explains the idea of transmitting memories to Jonas and transmits the first memory to him, that of snow.	The old Receiver, too, has pale eyes. The differences between the general Community and the Giver's environment are emphasized. Most striking to Jonas is the fact that the Giver can turn off the speaker.
11	Jonas experiences sledding downhill with excitement, pleasure and peace, and he receives the memory of sunshine, accompanied by sunburn. He learns the words for these experiences. The Giver warns him about coming pains.	Transmitting the memories lightens the burden on the Giver, but it exhausts him at the same time. Jonas becomes aware of a world beyond his own. Climate Control made the growing of crops and delivery easier when society went to "Sameness." Through these new experiences Jonas learns words that no longer exist in his Community. The word "Giver" is introduced.
12	When Jonas listens to Fiona's reports of her training at the House of the Old, her appearance seems to change. The Giver explains this startling change by transmitting the memory of the color red. The Giver transmits the memory of a rainbow, which makes Jonas see all colors.	Fiona reveals that the Old are punished just like little children are. The Community gave up color when they got rid of differences and went to Sameness. But the genetic scientists have not been able so far to get completely rid of color (Fiona has red hair).

Chapter	Content	Observations
13	The memory of an elephant hunt with all its bloody details is transmitted to Jonas. Jonas wonders about the far distance, Elsewhere, and wants to relieve the Giver of his pain. Jonas learns that the whole knowledge of the world is contained in books. The Giver is increasingly critical of the Community: the Elders do not ask his advice often enough and the teachers know nothing.	The Community does not dare let people make choices of their own, as making choices for them is much safer. Spouses and jobs are chosen for people. Jonas becomes more and more angry at his friends because they do not share his growing awareness. There are no animals (mammals) in the Community. Old people without young children are sent to live with the Childless Adults. Books are forbidden to the rest of the society, even to the Giver's spouse. The Givers' loneliness is revealed. Jonas' interest in the land beyond the bridge is mentioned.
14	Jonas experiences pain when he breaks his leg in another sledding memory and hears that there is more pain waiting for him: the pain of destruction. The newchild Gabriel is soothed by Jonas' transmission of nice memories to him.	Jonas' Community seems to be a largely pain-free society. Possession of the memories is to give the Receiver the wisdom necessary to make the right decisions. Release of a newchild must be carried out by Jonas' father.
15	The memory of war is transmitted. The Giver asks Jonas' forgiveness for passing on this experience.	Death is mentioned (twice) for the first time.
16	In another memory Jonas sees a family celebrating a holiday (somewhat similar to Christmas). He experiences feelings of warmth, happiness and love. He is reprimanded for lack of precision of language when he asks about love at home. This makes him question the norms of his society more and think of change. His first protest is his refusal to take the pills.	Gabriel receives many memories from Jonas. Besides the Giver, Gabriel is the only one he can share them with. The speakers on the walls also serve as microphones with someone possibly listening to what is said. Open fires are forbidden in Jonas' society.
17	Jonas is angry with some children who are playing war games, but his attempts to explain are in vain because the children don't have the memories of war, literally do not know what they are doing.	Jonas contemplates the difference between the socially engineered "feelings" of his society and "real" feelings. Real feelings can't be "talked away"; they must be felt. He experiences increasing estrangement from his comrades. Jonas' father tells him that if a person is released, somebody from Elsewhere comes to take this person away.
18	When he asks, Jonas is informed about the failure of the previous Receiver, Rosemary, who could not cope with the memories of loneliness and loss, and after five weeks asked to be released. The Giver warns Jonas to stay away from the river.	Jonas still adheres to the basic decision that he will have to bear the memories for the whole Community. The Giver's increasing bitterness and his premonition that he might lose Jonas are revealed.

Chapter	Content	Observations
19	Jonas witnesses the release of a twin performed by his father and comes to the terrible conclusion that his father killed this baby. The Giver tells Jonas that he watched a tape of Rosemary's release. She had asked to be allowed to inject herself with the deadly poison.	Dramatic turning point prepares Jonas' plan to escape.
20	Jonas is devastated by his terrible discovery. He does not go home that night. Jonas and the Giver make an elaborate plan for Jonas to escape on the day of the following ceremony. The Giver, however, will stay and help the Community to get over their confusion.	The terrible premonition that other people in the Community may also be lying is confirmed: his father had lied to him. Music does not exist in Jonas' world.
21	Jonas is forced to flee the following night because he is informed that Gabriel is scheduled for release after crying during the night of Jonas' absence. He takes Gabriel with him. Having to hide from airplanes, they move at night – and, with the help of soothing memories – sleep during the day.	
22	Having arrived in a different world, where life is less easy and predictable, Jonas has terrible doubts about whether they will be able to survive.	Jonas is only concerned about saving Gabriel.
23	Despite the fading of the memories, Jonas finally manages to transmit the feeling of warmth into Gabriel. When they arrive at the top of a hill, Jonas finds a sled and, hearing music, they ride downhill.	Jonas feels that at the bottom of the hill there are people celebrating something important and waiting for him and also for a baby to arrive …

3. Point of view

The novel is told in the third person, but not from an omniscient point of view. The author presents the story from the perspective of Jonas, whose eyes are slowly being opened. Lois Lowry restricts the information the reader gets to what Jonas sees, hears, feels, thinks and learns. When asked about the choice of the third-person point of view in *The Giver*, Lois Lowry gave the following answer:

> I never consciously chose a point of view. Some books, or stories, seem to need to be written from one viewpoint, some from another. I can go back, later, sometimes, and identify why a point of view works for a particular book. *Rabble Starkey*, for example, had to be in the first person because the voice was unique and it had to be told in that voice, not an authorial voice.
>
> It never occurred to me to write *The Giver* in anything other than the third person. I think the concreteness, the impersonality of the world I was attempting to create required the limited omniscient viewpoint. Limited because I needed, as well, to be inside Jonas' head. In addition, *The Giver* could not be written in the first person and retain the ambiguity of its ending. I know a lot of people would like the ending more spelled out and wrapped up nicely; but I prefer it to be open-ended; and it's almost impossible to do that if you're writing in the first person.

(Quoted on the site of the International Public Library in 1998:
http://www.ipl.org/div/askauthor/Lowry.html)

II Teaching the novel *The Giver*

1. The teaching unit

This teaching unit is conceived for 16 to 20 lessons, which do not have to be single lessons. Indeed, it would be advantageous if it could be taught as a whole in a one- or two-week unit or in the form of a project, which per se is usually more open and more student-centered. But even if we teach single lessons, as most of us still do, we can get our students involved and create room for them to realize their own ideas. These ideas are often surprising and unpredictable and worth pursuing, but still, we have to make a plan in order to inspire the students and to give them direction, focus and information about the expected results of their work.

As the overview of my teaching unit shows, I suggest working on several levels:

After the introductory part (3–4 lessons), in which students are given room to air their first reactions and in which they are guided to look at the characters and the society they live in more closely, students get information on how to continue reading and responding. In this phase one could ask students to choose from a number of possible tasks:

a) Choice of reading tasks (Copymaster 3). The list of chosen tasks will be displayed in the classroom during the whole unit.

b) Choice of whether to write a reading journal or a film or audio-script as a homework project.

After the first phase students will get a copy of the overview of the teaching unit (pp. 14–16) so that they know what is expected of them at any time. While the students are reading, they will not get new assignments (unless the class decides to change the schedule).

The second and the third parts of the teaching unit both emphasize writing. Whereas in the second phase writing is used to clarify one's own ideas and to organize one's thoughts to be able to communicate with classmates and the teacher more effectively, in the third part the students are asked to communicate with the outside world. E-mail partners, or anonymous web pages and the like are the correspondents here.

Why do I stress writing so much? It seems to me that writing in the communicative approach to language teaching has been ignored to a large extent in the classroom, whereas it has remained the main basis for the formal evaluation of students' abilities. It seems unfair to me that students are expected to know how to write exam papers without being instructed on how a good paper should be organized and designed and which steps must be taken to achieve this aim. In our writing assignments we should try to help students to write good papers and we should encourage them to emulate Lois Lowry's clear language and her extraordinary imagination.

2. An overview

Theme	Activity	Text, Material, Class Organization, Homework
Phase 1: Getting into the novel: Chapters 1–3		
Chapter 1: The characters (1 lesson)	Two possibilities: 1. Students (S) listen to Chapter 1 in class, collect information on characters and formulate expectations or questions. 2. In groups of six or twelve, S speculate on relationships among characters after having read role cards and looked at the cover; then they may listen to Chapter 1.	Audio recording of Chapter 1 (available for download via online code m33e6f) Pair work: cards, paper, one for each pair to be hung up in class. Group work role cards (Copymaster 1, p. 36) Questions on paper to be hung up in the classroom
Chapter 2: The Community (1 lesson)	Listen to Chapter 2. Students find information on the Community.	Audio recording of Chapter 2 (available for download via online code m33e6f) Pair or group work Worksheet: the Community (Worksheet 2, p. 37)
Chapter 3: Roles and rules in the Community (1 lesson)	Listen to Chapter 3. Roles and rules are discussed and results summarized on board. Introduction of reading tasks.	Audio recording of Chapter 3 (available for download via online code m33e6f) List of reading tasks with names assigned is hung up in classroom (Copymaster 3, p. 38). HW: read Chapters 4–8
Transition: How to go on reading		
Classroom instructions and discussion of worksheets (1 lesson)	Core vocabulary How to keep: – a vocabulary notebook – a reading journal	Info and worksheet on core vocabulary (Copymaster 4 & 5, pp. 39–40) Info sheet: how to keep a reading journal (Copymaster 6, p. 41)

ISBN 978-3-12-578137-5

Theme	Activity	Text, Material, Class Organization, Homework
Phase 2: **Selected in-class activities: Chapters 4–8**		
Dramatization of Chapter 5: Dream-telling ritual (1 lesson)	Act out the scene.	Sample script for screenplay (Copymaster 7, p. 42) *HW: Read up to chapter 15; while reading focus on the rules for Jonas, the new Receiver (see Ch. 9, p.58).*
Chapters 7 & 8 **The Ceremony of Twelve** (2 lessons)	Write the scene as a script and act it out. Introduce a narrator who sums up the event at the beginning. Choose a character that you want to play and act out the scene.	Dramatic structure (Copymaster 8, p. 43) Model scene for the teacher (Copymaster 9, p. 44)
Chapters 9–15: Jonas as the new Receiver and the transmission of memories (2 lessons)	1. Chapter 9: discussion of Jonas' rules, especially the last rule on the list: "You may lie." 2. Evaluate the memories and their specific meaning for Jonas and the Community.	List of rules and their impact on Jonas (on transparency) (Copymaster 10, p. 45) Worksheet on memories (Copymaster 11, p. 46) *HW: Finish reading the book.*
Chapters 16 & 18: The Giver's favorite memory: the concept of love and Jonas' increasing anger (2 lessons)	Group work: Compare and contrast: 1. "Love" in the Giver's memory and "love" in the Community; 2. Jonas and Rosemary.	Info sheet "Writing tips I" (Copymaster 12, p. 47)
Chapter 19: Jonas observes a release (1 lesson)	Write what Jonas observes and feels when his father releases the twin.	Info sheet "Writing tips I" (Copymaster 12, p. 47)
Transition: Chapters 20–23		
Summary writing or: **Finding a new ending** (1 lesson)	Write a summary of the last four chapters. Write a different ending for the story.	Info sheet "Writing tips II" (Copymaster 13, p. 48)

ISBN 978-3-12-578137-5

Theme	Activity	Text, Material, Class Organization, Homework
Phase 3: Post-reading activities		
Answers to questions raised at beginning of unit. **Personal responses in the form of a poem** (1 lesson). **Reading tasks and writing about the Community** (2 lessons).	Creating a chain poem	Papers containing predictions made in lesson 1 hanging on classroom wall Sample poem (Copymaster 14, p. 49) Describe, analyze and evaluate the Community, (Copymaster 15, p. 50)
The "30 Minutes" Talk Show (1 lesson) **Writing a book review**	Students discuss the advantages and disadvantages of the two societies. Write your own online review: – short summary (synopsis) – personal recommendation	Copymaster 16, p. 51 Sample reviews from amazon.com (Copymaster 17, p. 52)
Writing a film review	Watch the film; compare novel and film	DVD, Compare film and ending; write a film review (Copymaster 18 & 19, pp. 53–54)
Examination paper / Oral exams (2 lessons)	Different assignments	Copymasters 20 & 21, pp. 55–56)

ISBN 978-3-12-578137-5

3. Getting into the novel

Due to novel's the limited point of view and the alien nature of the society portrayed, even good students will at first find the novel confusing. It is therefore very important to make sure that our students receive careful guidance. If they do not get a good introduction, they might not feel confident enough to complete the increasingly difficult tasks later on. Therefore I suggest that in the first three or four lessons the teacher should make sure that everyone understands the general situation of the characters in the first three chapters, their role in the Community and the rules under which they live.

3.1 The characters (Chapter 1)

Goals: Students are introduced to the novel and their interest is to be aroused. The following are possibilities for the first lesson:

Audio files available for download at www.klett-sprachen.de

Enter online code m33e6f or scan QR-Code

1st possibility: Listen to the first chapter and ask students to write down their individual or group questions and speculations, which are hung up in class so that they can be referred to again at the end of the unit. Also the cover and the blurb may help to formulate speculations on the content of the story.

Notebooks

2nd possibility: The teacher hands out role cards (Copymaster 1, p. 36) to groups of six or twelve (if there are twelve students in the group, two students get the same role card so that they can help each other out) who are to guess from this information what the book might be about. Each student (or each pair) reads the information and in their own words gives the information to the other members of the group. When the students' characters start interacting with each other, the activity becomes a real role play.

Copymaster 1, p. 36

3.2 The Community (Chapter 2)

Goals: Students find out as much as they can about the Community while listening to or reading Chapter 2 and complete Worksheet 2 (p. 37)

Worksheet 2, p. 37

Audio files available for download at www.klett-sprachen.de

Enter online code m33e6f

or scan QR-Code

Possible solution to Worksheet 2:

Family units	Couples apply for a child who is expected to fit into the already established family unit.
Rules	Rules must not be broken. However, the rule that a child may not ride a bike before he/she turns nine and receives one at the Ceremony is almost always broken. Committees sometimes change rules.
Ceremony (of Twelve)	This takes place every December, lasts two days, is exciting because it brings great changes. Each new-child (child born in that year) is named, becomes a One and is assigned to a family unit. Each of the 50 children in each year group has a number.

Ceremony (of Twelve) *continued*	The Twelves get their lifetime assignments, which may be appealed against. After the Ceremony people lose track of their age. Children no longer spend time with their age groups but with assignment or work groups.
The Elders	Leaders of the Community; committee is in charge of rules and assignments, which they select after observing each child carefully and after talking with the instructors.
The Receiver	Most important Elder who makes final decisions on rules. Lives and works alone.
Assignments/ Training	Each child gets his/her assignment at the age of twelve, according to his/her aptitudes and inclinations. Assignments are made at the Ceremony and no one is allowed to know it in advance (rule). Assignments mentioned: Nurturer, Laborer, Doctor, Engineer.
School/Play/ Volunteer work	The children's time is divided into school time, recreation time and volunteer hours.

3.3 Roles and rules (chapter 3)

Board

Audio files available for download at www.klett-sprachen.de

Enter online code m33e6f

or scan QR-Code

Goals: Find out more about the Community, e.g.:

→ its roles (jobs, assignments for children, adults)
→ its rules
→ its appearance (geography, city plan – not yet presented in detail; will be presented by a group of students later)

This is what the board could look like:

Roles	Rules
Birthmothers: • get good food, have gentle exercise lessons, play games, amuse themselves while waiting for the children to be born • a maximum of three births in three years, after that they become Laborers till they enter the House of the Old; they never get to see the newchildren **Other assignments:** Nurturer, Speaker (making announcements from an office)	• mentioning differences between individuals is considered rude • there are no mirrors • announcements from loud-speakers: hair ribbons are to be tied neatly at all times (for young females) • objects are not to be removed from the recreation areas • snacks are to be eaten at school, not taken home • apologies must be made for mistakes (for everybody)

Roles	Rules
	• citizens are reminded of rules through loudspeakers so that they feel guilt, shame, remorse ...
Volunteers: Children start their volunteer hours at the age of eight; one place is the Birthing Center, another the Nurturing Center.	
Other • people ride bikes and put bikes into bike ports • loudspeakers seem to be every-where	

The teacher might want to ask the students to find out in what way objects and people are described in this chapter. The students would then find out that eyes are described as being pale or dark (**23** 7–8) and that an apple is described as being of a nondescript shade, just like Jonas' tunic (**26** 7–8). There is no reference to color anywhere.

4. Preparing home reading and studying

After these initial activities, it is time for the students to read by themselves, each focusing on a specific topic. They can work at their own pace within the scheduled time and have to have their tasks ready for the post-reading activities. Except for this and the required reading there is no additional homework.

4.1 Reading task selection

Copymaster 3, p. 38

To give students a real choice, it is important to find many assignments from which they can choose (Copymaster 3, p. 38). Teachers could limit the number of students that select one particular assignment. For example, scriptwriting cannot be done by one person alone; on the other hand the group should not consist of more than 5–6 scriptwriters, since there might be too much dissent on choosing scenes.

The reading tasks will be discussed in class at a later stage. Possible solutions are presented in chapter 6.2, p. 27ff.

4.2 Vocabulary

Learning vocabulary is a highly individual matter. There are many ways of learning vocabulary. Research has shown that words are best learnt in context. Some students might have retained some words already just by reading the novel, but maybe the words have not yet been stored in their memory. Therefore I suggest that students actively try to memorize words by organizing them in different contexts.

Copymasters 4 & 5, pp. 39–40

The **word list** on Copymaster 4 (p. 39) will help students to talk and write about the novel. The words are given in alphabetical order. The words marked with an asterisk (*) were created by the author or have been given a special meaning and need only be understood in the context of the novel.

The word list can be used in different ways – see **learning strategies** on Copymaster 5:

1. Students put the words into different **categories**. The Copymaster suggests categories, which, however, can be changed, reduced, expanded ...

2. Students make various **mind maps** with different headwords.
If students like mind maps they should arrange the words in chunks, not only in single words. An example is given on Copymaster 5, p. 40.

3. Another way of making use of the list: while working on the assignments students **tick words** that they have used in their text. They are encouraged to use as many words as possible from the list to enlarge their vocabulary.

4. Students **expand the list** by adding translations, example sentences, synonyms, antonyms, etc.

These strategies will help you cater to the individual needs and abilities of the students in your group.

4.3 Reading journal

Asking students to keep a reading journal is a good way of giving them room for individual responses, not only when reading and writing in their mother tongue, but also when a foreign language is involved. Unlike a diary, which is private, a journal contains ideas that may be shared with others.

Copymaster 6, p. 41

Copymaster 6 (p. 41) provides a list of ideas students could use in their reading journals. You might want to discuss these in class to make students become interested in keeping a reading journal.

5. Selected in-class activities

Not every chapter will be discussed at great length in the classroom, but certain parts have to be highlighted because of their thematic or stylistic importance.

Chapters 5, 7 and 8 are dramatic highlights, which can well be transformed into a script. One reason for using scriptwriting early in the unit is that some students might become interested in dramatizing the novel by themselves once they have been introduced to the method.

5.1 Novel into drama: Writing scripts in Part 1 (Chapters 4–8)

5.1.1 Chapter 5: Jonas' first stirrings

Chapter 5 is very interesting, especially for adolescent students experiencing their own sexual development, as it depicts the Community's way of dealing with developing sexuality.

Much shorter than the chapter itself, the screen or radio play will only focus on Jonas' dream, which is crucial to his development as he later stops taking the pills altogether, a step towards his increasingly critical attitude to his Community.
At this point, you can either get your students to write a script themselves, or use the one provided on Copymaster 7 (p. 42) and act out the scene in class.

Copymaster 7, p. 42

Write a script (for a screenplay) of the scene in Chapter 5, where Jonas relates his first stirrings.

Act out the scene in Chapter 5, where Jonas relates his first stirrings. Feel free to make changes to the script provided.

5.1.2 Chapters 7–8: The Ceremony of Twelve

Chapter 8 is the first climax (Plot Point I) of the novel, as it represents the most important day in Jonas' life, the day he was so apprehensive about at the beginning of the novel.

As Chapter 7 deals with the first day of the Ceremony, both chapters can be combined by introducing a narrator who sums up Chapter 7. The scene may either serve as yet another writing model for students, or it can be created by students themselves after the previous model. From this point on, one group could work independently on writing a film or radio script with the intention of having the whole group perform it. Being very much used to drama through the media, students will have little difficulty in selecting the most dramatic parts of the novel and joining them together. They will easily see that Jonas' witnessing the release of the twin in Chapter 19 leads to Plot Point II, his decision to escape with Gabriel. Initially, the scriptwriters should work closely with the text and later decide which portions of the text are to be shortened, summarized, dropped or expanded so that the dramatic parts are highlighted.

According to Syd Field's *The Screenwriter's Workbook*, a script should consist of three acts. You could hand out Copymaster 8 to the scriptwriter group, discuss it in class after the whole novel has been read or have the scriptwriters figure out the dramatic tension in the novel, which is highlighted in the two plot points.

Copymasters 8 & 9, pp. 43–44

Copymaster 9 contains a sample script. The scene can easily be acted out in class. Students who do not have a role can take over the part of the whole Community.

5.2 Spoken and written interaction in Part 2: Jonas in the role of the new Receiver and the transmission of memories (Chapters 9–18)

Chapter 9 forms the transition from the first climax, Jonas' assignment, to his upcoming training, which confronts him with extreme concepts and feelings that he has never experienced in this Community of Sameness. The following aspects could be emphasized, as they are extremely important for the further understanding of the novel and as they will keep the students' attention at a high level.

- in **Chapter 9** the study of the rules and Jonas' reaction to them, especially the upsetting question arising from the rule "you may lie";
- in **Chapters 10–15** the various memories and their impact on Jonas, leading to a better understanding of a society trying to get rid of inequality and difficulties by discarding differences, history and strong feelings;
- in **Chapter 16** the Giver's favorite memory of love;
- and finally, in **Chapter 19**, Jonas' terrible confrontation with his father's lie, a lie that hid the fact that "release" is actually murder. Jonas' witnessing of the twin's release is the second climax of the novel and it leads to the denouement in **Chapter 20:** his decision to escape.

5.2.1 Talking about Jonas' rules (Worksheet 10)

Worksheet 10, p. 45

Goals: Students find out how Jonas reacts to the rules set out for him. They complete Worksheet 10 (ideally including evidence from the text).

Possible solutions to Worksheet 10:

Chapter 9: Rules for the new Receiver	**Jonas' reactions**
Go to your training every day immediately after school. (**58** 10)	He is worried about having no recreation time, no time for play or to ride his bike; he fears he may lose his friends. (**58** 23–29)
Go home immediately after your training. (**58** 11)	He accepts this. (**58** 27–28)
You may be rude: i.e. ask any citizen any question and you will receive answers. (**58** 13)	As he is used to courtesy, this rule startles him, makes him feel awkward. He can't imagine asking anyone an intimate question. (**59** 1–7)
Don't discuss your training with anybody, not even parents and Elders. (**58** 16)	No immediate reaction, but in the course of the novel Jonas experiences this as a burden.
You must not tell anyone about your dreams any more. (**58** 18)	Not a problem, as he dreams very rarely. The thought that he might have to lie to his parents if he dreams is unnerving to him. (**59** 8–13)
Except for illness and injury that has nothing to do with your training you must not ask for medicine. (**58** 19)	Because he is used to quick pain relief the instant something happens, it unnerves him when he thinks of having to suffer pain,

Chapter 9: Rules for the new Receiver	**Jonas' reactions**
	but he is relieved when he realizes that he may ask for medication against pain unrelated to his training. He can also continue taking the "anti-Stirrings" pill. He is worried about possible "indescribable" pain in his training. (**59** 16–34)
You may not apply for release. (**58** 21)	He does not react to this rule at all, as he cannot imagine when or why he might want to ask for it. (**59** 35–36)
You may lie. (**58** 22)	This rule seems to be the most troubling to him. He thinks that everybody might have gotten this same rule at the age of 12, so that everybody was allowed to lie from that age on. But now he can be rude and ask someone whether or not he/she is lying. (**60** 1–25) (For discussion: Lack of language precision can also be a form of lying: e.g. the use of "starve" vs. "be hungry"; cf. Orwell's remarks on "Newspeak". See file download at www.klett-sprachen.de, online code hy5yx7)

File download at www.klett-sprachen.de
online code: hy5yx7

5.2.2 Filling in a form: Jonas, the new Receiver of Memory

Worksheet 11, p. 46

Worksheet 11 (p. 46) can be handed out before students read chapters 10–18 to help them to read closely and focus on the memories while reading. Of course, the information can always be collected in class so that you have concrete results at the end of a lesson.

Possible Solution to Worksheet 10:

Memory	**Impact on Jonas**	**Why abolished/comments**
snow (hill)	• Jonas, sitting on sled gliding downhill feels cold, soft, painless pinpricks, sees "a bright, whirling torrent of crystals" (**67** 29)	• climate control: snow made growing food difficult • weather (including sunshine) was abolished
sunshine	• warmth pervading his body: pleasant all-over sensation (word for sunshine comes to him spontaneously)	• hills made conveyance of goods unwieldy (**69** 29 ff.)

Memory	Impact on Jonas	Why abolished/comments
sunburn	• skin stinging, sharp pain in the crease of his arm (Giver tells him the word for it (**71** 28)	
color	• sees color and shades of color • seeing color means gaining wisdom • Jonas wants to decide between clothes of different colors (**79** 18)	• abolished so there will be no visible differences, but genetic scientists, who are still trying to solve the last details of the problem, have not quite mastered Sameness (**77** 33 ff.) • people have to be prevented from making wrong choices (**80** 11)
animals (elephants)	• experiences elephants being hunted with guns (a new word) for their ivory tusks in African bushlands and is appalled by the shouts of the blood-thirsty hunters • overwhelmed by the perception of a new red (blood), the shouts of greed and the elephant's sound of grief and rage	• no explanation offered for the abolition of animals (mammals) • (students might speculate on possible reasons)
bone fracture; pain	Jonas endures terrible pain; he cries and vomits.	creation of a "painless" society
colorful memories of nature	memories of pleasure lessen the pain a little: • brisk sail on a blue-green lake • meadow with colorful wild flowers • orange sunset behind mountains (**89** 9)	
suffering of the past: destruction **hunger** **warfare**	• sight of the neglected and unfed causes spasms in his stomach (**89** 12) • Jonas sees a boy of his own age dying, begging for water; • hears, sees and smells other men and horses die, hears sound of cannons (**95**)	• evils of the past abolished; • memory gives wisdom to the Giver; • knowing about hunger made him advise against more births (over-population), which in the past had led to hunger and warfare (**89**). • function of Receiver: lift burden from the Community (**90** 32)
love: families, holidays, happiness	Jonas is filled with a feeling of happiness and warmth when he sees a "complete" family, including grandparents, celebrate something. (**97**)	• it is impractical with the Old living in the same family and not being taken care of well enough; • real candles and fireplaces are risky (**99**)

5.2.3 Writing about The Giver's favorite memory: love (Chapters 16 and 18)

Copymaster 12, p. 47

Students are given the following tasks along with an infosheet on *Writing* which also contains some useful phrases and expressions (Copymaster 12, p. 47).

***Task 1:** After reading these chapters, write a "Love is" poem about the different kinds of love that are expressed here. You may use words from the text.*
*In the book 'love' is mentioned on pp.: **19** 1, **46** 21, **98** 37, **99** 7, **99** 18, **100** 4–23, **101** 19, **119** 2, **124** 27, **132** 8, **134** 20, **136** 18 .*

***Task 2:** Compare and contrast Jonas and Rosemary.*

Possible solutions:

Task 1

In the Community	**For the Giver and Jonas**
Love is politeness	Love is like fire
Love is hidden with pills	Love is not precise
Love is obsolete	Love is taking risks
Love is meaningless	Love is no more pills
Love is dangerous	Love is celebration
Love is forbidden	Love is joy
…	Love is caring
	Love is heart-breaking
	Love is feeling

Task 2
Similarities and differences

The two characters Rosemary and Jonas are **similar** in the following ways:

Jonas and Rosemary were **both** selected to be Receivers of Memory.
They are both intelligent, brave, eager to learn and see new things. (**However,** it is said that Jonas can see beyond, which is not said about Rosemary.)
They are also **similar in that** they receive positive and negative memories and don't want to be spared although the memories are hard to endure.
Like Rosemary, Jonas is happy experiencing joy and love, and they both are devastated by the negative memories. **However**, the Giver chooses different memories for each of them. Whereas the memory of loss of a child is transmitted to Rosemary, Jonas has to endure physical pain and war. **Yet** he endures the pain (**although** at one point he says he wants his childhood back). **Like** Rosemary, he does not want to be spared and above all does not ask the Chief Elder for release. **Instead of** suffering and being self-destructive he takes action when he realizes that Gabe's life is in danger.
Whilst Rosemary gave up, so that her selection was considered a failure, Jonas fights the system and wins in the end.

5.2.4 Jonas' terrible discovery: release = murder

Chapter 19 is the second climax in the book, in which Jonas finds out the truth about release and that it is only a euphemism for killing, even murder.
The students who focused on the issue of release in the reading assignments now make their presentations, in which they explain to the class what release means,

what a release ceremony is like and who in the Community is released. The other students take notes.

5.3 Part 3: Chapters 20–23 (Jonas' escape)

5.3.1 Summarizing the ending

Copymaster 13, p. 48

Remind students of the basic rules of writing summaries (see also Copymaster 13, p. 48). Then ask them to summarize the ending.

5.3.2 Writing a different ending

Lois Lowry herself reports that many people have written to her because they are either dissatisfied with the ending or want her to explain the ending to them. However, she refuses to do so. On the other hand, she admits that the escape part feels a little hurried to her. If you think the book needs a different ending or that the whole ending needs to be rewritten, have students write one.

You could also tell students about *Son*, the last book of *The Giver Quartet* in which the author has finally written an ending herself. (cf., p. 93 f.)

6. Post-reading classroom activities

6.1 Creative writing: Writing a poem

Copymaster 14, p. 49

The students are to write down ten words from the book that come to their mind (in 60 seconds) underneath each other in the middle of an empty page (or on the back of Copymaster 14, p. 49).

For example:

Giver
Receiver
Ceremony
release
memory
sameness
difference
colors
snow
war

Then they are to connect these words with each other by completing the lines. No rhyme is necessary. For example, like this:

The **Giver** selects an innocent 12-year-old to become
the **Receiver** of all the past memories
at a **Ceremony**.
In his training Jonas loses his innocence when he learns that people
are **released**.
Other **memories** make him realize that
sameness, not
difference is wanted in the state.
No **colors**,
No **snow**,
No **war**.
Is this what we all want?

The "poems" are collected and read by the teacher so that rhythm and sound are stressed. Various perceptions are compared and discussed in class. Some may be hung up in the classroom if the writers agree.

6.2 Describing and analyzing the Community (initial reading tasks)

Copymaster 15, p. 50

Now is the time to finally refer back to the reading tasks that each student chose at the beginning of the unit. Students are asked to present their findings in an outline or table form on an overhead transparency or in an electronic format, if you have an appropriate classroom setup. Students can take notes in their reading journals or notebooks, or use Copymaster 15, p. 50.

Possible outcome: refers back to list of reading tasks on Copymaster 3, p. 38

Themes/tasks	Results
The Community	Population: The Community probably consists of about 4,000 inhabitants, if there is a life expectancy of 80 (?) years, which, multiplied by 50 (birthrate per year), amounts to 4,000. (This being a Utopian society, life expectancy could well be higher, say 120. Still, it would be a Community that is not overwhelmingly big.) There are about 1,000 families, each family unit consisting of a maximum of four members. Citizens: The Community consists of: pre-schoolers, school children (volunteers), children in training, full adults (with family units), childless adults (including adults with grown children) and the Old. Recreation and play: Children have regulated recreation time in which they can play. One of the harmless games is: good guys against bad guys, which ends when everybody lies "posed in freakish postures on the ground" (**104** 9). Jonas identifies it as a war game. School and training: Teachers are called "instructors", who are well-trained like the rest of the Community, but, according to the Giver, "know nothing" (**84** 34; see also **85** 5 ff.); they teach necessary skills in language and communication, commerce and industry, science and technology, civil procedures and government (**73** 25 ff.);

Themes/tasks	Results
	students learn about the latest technology; Jonas has learnt scientific data on how the brain works, but nothing about the importance of memory (**84** 29 ff.). There are no books except reference books and the Community Volume that contains descriptions of Community facilities and a Book of Rules. Students have to memorize rules even after they have started their adult training. Formal training will end soon for 12-year-olds (**102** 11). People's looks: Everybody has dark eyes, except four people who seem to have special gifts; they have pale eyes. Everybody seems to wear tunics; in the House of the Old the volunteers wear smocks; the Caretakers of the Old wear uniforms. Rules and regulations: Rules for the whole Community must be learned by school-children; there is a Book of Rules (**36** 12). Minor and major rules: minor rules (like riding a bike before a child is 9) may be broken and a breach is not strictly prosecuted, but for breaking major rules repeatedly (3 times) the death penalty ("release") may be imposed. Giver and Receiver each have a different set of rules (**83** 15). Relationship between authorities and citizens: Loudspeakers in every dwelling remind the Community of the rules, admonishing them when a rule is not obeyed (which means that the "speakers" can also be used to spy on people). People are obviously trained well in the family unit and conditioned in such a way that they do not need much admonishing. The Committee of Elders makes rules for the Community to prevent them from making wrong choices (**80** 11). Housing: Every family lives in the same kind of dwelling, which is furnished with standard furniture, in contrast to the luxuriously furnished and decorated Annex building, where Jonas' training takes place (**62** 12 ff.). The dwellings seem to be in a separate residential area, set apart from the Central Plaza and the public buildings (office buildings, Auditorium; cf. **29** 4–9). Government: The Community is governed (controlled) by a Committee of Elders who are set apart from the rest of the Community (e.g. they wear different clothes than the rest of the Community; **63** 8). History: The Community has only one generation of memories (**76** 28), which means there is no history. Work: Work is assigned according to a person's abilities and inclinations. Despite rumors to the contrary, there is no concrete evidence of anyone ever disliking the work assigned to them. Despite the general egalitarian ideology of the Community, certain positions/people are looked down upon (e.g. the night-crew nurturers **14** 3; birthmothers **24** 8–9; see also Larissa's remarks about differences **32** 4–8).
Ceremonies	Each year in December the Ceremony, attended by the whole Community, is celebrated. The Ceremony can be subdivided into a number of different ceremonies: • Ceremony for the Ones: newchildren are named and placed in family units. • Ceremony of Seven: children receive their first real jackets with buttons on the front. • Ceremony of Eight: girls stop wearing hair ribbons; all start volunteer hours. • Ceremony of Nine: children receive and are allowed to ride their first bicycles. • Ceremony of Twelve: lifetime work assignments are given. There are also unscheduled holidays, but rarely (**102**). Release ceremony: a non-public ceremony is held when a person "dies" (**31** 30–31). Ceremony of Loss in the rare case of accidental death (**41** 5–10).

Themes/tasks	Results
Landscape/ architecture/ sound and col-our/traffic/ technology	**Landscape:** Lawn around Central Plaza, bushes on the riverbank (**79**); agricultural fields beyond the Community boundary, without color, in "flat and hueless shade" (**79** 8–9) A bridge spans the river, to be crossed only by people on official business (**85** 37). Beyond, other Communities can be visited; these are very similar with their flat, well-ordered fields for agriculture. **Architecture:** Dwellings all the same, with bike port next to house, no doors locked (**61** 32); Central Plaza, schools, Childcare Center near small offices and factories (**29** 5 ff.). House of the Old (rest home) adjacent to Annex building where the Giver resides; Hall of Open Records with flower beds (**80** 24); no shops (food is delivered to people's houses by laborers) **Sounds:** terrifying noise from plane (Ch. 1); loudspeakers in every dwelling; people have gentle voices, there is no music **Color:** no color, only shades of gray **Traffic:** Everybody rides bikes with nameplates on them (**61** 7). Vehicles are driven only by work crews. There are cargo planes. **Technology:** The Community possesses modern military technology, like airplanes equipped with heat-seeking devices which can identify body warmth (**129** 7 f.).
Other Commu-nities and the outside world – Elsewhere	The surrounding Communities look essentially the same as Jonas' Community. The only difference: slightly altered styles of dwellings, slightly different school schedules; minor differences in the rules they follow. Land in the far distance beyond other Communities (**86**). The Community is separated from other Communities by a river. But what lies beyond these other Communities, where roads become narrower and where wildlife exists (**130** 2 ff.), is not Elsewhere yet. Jonas only reaches Elsewhere when he sleds down the hill to the final destination, a place that holds the future and the past (**136** 11 f.). Else-where is also the land of the unknown where the dead may go (**43** 34; **92** 5 ff.).
Characters	
Jonas	11, turning 12, a regular child who loves play and games, has a best friend, is attracted to a girl, is very considerate, which is a consequence of the general upbringing in the Community. He has the capacity "to see beyond", which means that he can momentarily perceive the true color of things like the apple (**26** 1–8), the faces of the people at the Ceremony (**54** 23–**25**), Fiona's hair (**74** 36 ff.), the sled (**77** 4), the books (**77** 13). He is apprehensive about the Ceremony of Twelve, where he is selected to be the new Receiver of Memory. He is introduced to all the memories of the world and learns that the apparent life of harmony in the Community is based on totalitarian measures (absence of choice, release – a euphemism for euthanasia – as a measure of social and biological control). When Gabriel is scheduled for release, Jonas flees with him, hoping to reach a place where Sameness does not reign.
Gabriel	Newchild = baby who does not grow as fast as he should or sleep as soundly as other babies. Has the same pale eyes as Jonas and The Giver. Causes trouble to the Community and is scheduled for release, which Jonas prevents by escaping from the Community and taking Gabriel with him. Is sensitive to memories that Jonas transmits to him in difficult situations.

Themes/tasks	Results
Lily	7–8 years old, lively, friendly, easy-going, a chatterbox, with an inclination to storytelling; likes Jonas and Gabriel, who she thinks is cute. Hates hair ribbons and waits for the day she can get rid of them and become more independent. Would like to be assigned the role of a Birthmother because she thinks they lead pleasant lives (**24** 9 ff.). Is looking forward to the ceremony when she receives her own bicycle. Breaks the rule of not riding a bike before the age of 9. But generally she obeys the rules and gets angry if someone does not (**12** 14 ff.).
Mother	Flat character; not much additional information about her after Chapter 2; holds an important job in the Department of Justice (**14** 29) – and therefore knows about the true meaning of release – speaks sharply when she reminds Lily that Birthmother is not an honored job (**24**), admonishes children to adhere to the rules, informs Jonas about the Stirrings and the medication he has to take; explains to Jonas what "precision of language" is (**100** 10 ff.).
Father	Nurturer, one of the most important jobs in the Community, looks after babies, gives them massages and baths (**31** 10), plays with them (**21** 13) before they are sent to their families. Shy and quiet (**18** 20), gentle, soft and caring. Feels guilty when he breaks minor rules like finding out Gabriel's name beforehand, but – except for the job – is a kind of role model for Jonas (**16** 25–**17** 1); was also 12 when his sister turned 9 (**17** 24-30); prevents Gabriel from being released by applying to care for him at home (**39** 28 ff.), but later votes in favor of Gabriel's release (**126** 8). Lives by the major rules of the Community and passes his training on, e.g. brings a discipline wand home when Gabriel starts walking (**106** 11 f.). Is selected to carry out release of a twin and kills it with an injection in his "caring" way (**115** 13 ff.); quite obviously lies to Jonas about the truth behind release; admonishes Jonas to use "precision of language" (**100** 6).
The Giver	Looks very old, his face wrinkled, eyes tired, with flesh around them dark and sagging (**63** 27 ff.). Diminishing energy; lives without his spouse who now lives with the Childless Adults (**82** 24). He is weary, disappointed in the Community, but at the beginning of Jonas' training still loyal. Wants to ask for release when Jonas is fully trained (**108** 11 f.). Becomes increasingly bitter (**117** 2–3) when he thinks of the failure of his previous trainee (**64** 20). His job is to transmit all the memories of the past that he has within him (**64** 26), which are the memories of the whole world (**65** 6 ff.). His job is very much honored, but does not give him much power (**70** 5 ff.). Is very rarely asked for advice by the Committee of Elders but knows that they need him to bear all the pain of the world for them (**83–84**).
Rosemary	The Giver's daughter who was once selected to be the Receiver but could not endure the pain of the memories and asked for release. Self-possessed, serene young woman, intelligent, eager to learn, with luminous eyes, enthusiastic about the new experience, responsible (**108–109**), but – in spite of the fact that The Giver tried to spare her bad memories – she could not endure the pain. He had to give her memories of pain because she did not want to be spared. Even at her own release she is brave and wants to inject herself with the deadly needle (**117** 4).

Themes/tasks	Results
Asher	11–12 , Jonas' best friend, always cheerful, has and has had problems using correct language, mixes up words that sound similar, and was disciplined for this when he was very young; often gets distracted. At the Ceremony he is assigned the job of Recreation Assistant in accordance with his disposition for play and is happy with his assignment. Later on he shows no understanding for Jonas' attitude towards the children's war game.
Fiona	11-12, Fiona spends many of her volunteer hours at the House of the Old (and is later assigned a job there), where she bathes the Old and learns much about administrative work, dietary rules, punishment for disobedience, occupational therapy, recreational activities, and medications (**74** 24 ff.). Not much is said about her feelings for Jonas, who is very affectionate and gentle (**108** 32) when he thinks of her. She rides home with Jonas from the House of the Old.
Language	Language is a means of conditioning people to accept the rules of the society, which ensures a smoothly running Community. Representatives of the Community are very serious and strict about "precision of language" (**48** 31). Words that have no equivalent in reality just do not exist or should not exist: ("love", "starve"; cf. **60** 10). Other words mean something utterly different: the word "animal" is used for someone who does not fit in (**12** 26). Words from the past are eliminated and replaced by others: wife/husband: spouse baby: Newchild family: family unit I'm starving: I'm hungry execution, murder: release to kill, execute, exterminate: to release
Release	It finally turns out that release is a euphemism for kill, execute, allow to commit suicide (**116** 15; **118** 35 f.). Old people are at some point (a specific age is not mentioned) scheduled for release (cf. **63** 34). People can also apply for release, i.e. commit assisted suicide. Fiona is one of the people who are trained in "the fine art of release" (**119** 6; an allusion to the essay "Murder Considered as One of the Fine Arts" by Thomas De Quincey). "Elsewhere" is the place where the released person may supposedly go (**43** 34; **92** 5 ff.). But release is also used as a punishment for people who have repeatedly committed crimes (**15** 3), or made serious mistakes like the pilot in ch. 1 (**10** 11; **14** 5 ff.). New-children who do not fit into the Community, who are in some way deficient, like Gabriel, who needs extra care (**13** 35) and has not gained enough weight, are called "inadequate" and released (**39** 29–33). Release of a Newchild always causes the Community a feeling of failure (**40** 10 f.) except when a twin is released, which must be done in accordance with the rules (**113** 7). When Rosemary could not bear all the pains which were transmitted to her, she applied for release (**110** 35 ff.), which is no longer possible for Jonas as her successor (**58** 21). Release ceremonies for the Old are public, but children are not allowed to attend. The procedure is described in detail (**31** 30–**33** 11). The word is used in a different sense in the book in connection with the "escaping" of memories. When Rosemary failed, her memories were released (**84** 7) to the Community (**86** 15).

6.3 The reading – discussing – writing connection

With the help of notes, tables, graphs, etc. on overhead transparencies, students present their findings in class. This should lead to class discussions as everybody has read the book and should have an opinion on the findings of the "specialists". Some details may have to be added, some statements may have to be corrected. Students are to take notes during the presentations and discussions. In the end they should produce essays (individually or in small groups) on the Community which deal with the following points:

- what the Community looks like;
- how the society is structured;
- what mechanisms for social control there are;
- how the people live (living conditions, jobs, education, housing, recreation, family planning, relationship ...);
- how individuals are treated;
- what role language plays;
- how death, history, memory, art, books, music ... are dealt with.

Copymaster 5, p. 40

In order to help students expand their vocabulary and vary their style, you should maybe make use of Copymaster 5 or create your own worksheet according to your students' needs.

6.4 The "30 Minutes" Talk Show

In a final panel discussion on the advantages and disadvantages of the society presented in *The Giver,* students are asked once again to use their newly acquired vocabulary and the ideas presented in the novel to discuss two different societies, their ideologies and their impact on the population.

The students take on a role and have to come up with arguments that fit their role and support their respective Community. Each role is taken over by at least two students so that someone who runs out of steam can be replaced by another. The students should be told that this panel discussion is to be broadcast as part of a program called "30 Minutes". In order to give the discussion a more realistic touch, you may consider doing it in the form of a TV talk show, which is in fact video-taped. Students tend to be better prepared for such a "show" as they take it more seriously.

Note that the role of host is often difficult to fill. If you feel you do not have a student who can be really effective in this role, you can take on the role yourself.

Copymaster 16, p. 51

There are several possible scenarios. Two possibilities are presented here (see also Copymaster 16, p. 51):

Scenario 1:
The Giver, Jonas and Rosemary meet with the Chief Elder, a Birthmother, Asher, Father or other characters from the book and try to persuade them to change their society.

Roles required: Host, Giver, Jonas, Rosemary, Chief Elder, Birthmother, Asher, Father, ...

Scenario 2:
The Giver, Jonas and Rosemary meet with representatives of our own contemporary society (e.g. a volunteer who works in the Third World, a conservative or a socialist politician, a nurse, a social worker), who see serious problems in our society and who advise them to go back to the Community.

Roles required: Host, Giver, Jonas, Rosemary, volunteer, conservative politician, socialist politician, nurse, social worker, …

Point out the useful phrases for agreeing and disagreeing on Copymaster 16 to students.

Here is a list of issues raised in the book which may also be discussed:

- **death:** euthanasia – eugenics – death penalty
- **culture:** memory – history – literature – books – art
- **education:** social engineering – child rearing – school – language
- **genetic engineering:** sameness – color – nature
- **society:** democracy – equality – totalitarian regime – hierarchy – control – war – safety
- **feelings:** love – pain – joy – excitement – passion – fear – hate – aggression
- **sex:** pregnancy – abortion – surrogate motherhood – family planning

6.5 Writing reviews

6.5.1 Writing a book review

The internet offers everybody the opportunity to publish his/her own texts and make them available to a worldwide audience, either on the school's web site or through other channels. Writing, which students usually regard as something boring that they have to do just for school, suddenly acquires a new dimension. In writing, one can communicate with the whole world and add one's own comments to what other people have written. This may be reason enough to avoid mistakes.

(Some reviewers on the internet, however, don't seem to be too concerned about this. You might therefore challenge your students to watch out for mistakes that even native speakers make something which will boost their confidence and they are quite likely to enjoy.) It might be a good idea to assign students to read several reviews of *The Giver* and then ask them to add their own. Most reviews start out with a synopsis (a one-sentence summary) of the whole book which you might ask your students to do, too, before they are allowed to add their view. Direct them to amazon.com or goodreads.com.

The reviews presented here (Copymaster 17, p. 52) are interesting as utterances of readers' personal feelings and, in addition to being mere sample reviews they can serve as the basis for a discussion of the entire novel. In the third review, for example, one can see how much the reader must have suffered while reading and that she/he seems to have hated this suffering rather than the book.

Copymaster 17, p. 52

6.5.2 Writing a film review

Copymasters 18 & 19, pp. 53–54

In 2014, the film *The Giver* was released. After this intense work with the novel, the film should be watched as a whole which should trigger lively classroom discussions. The students, who by now should know the book well, make notes about the differences between film and novel (Copymaster 18, p. 53) as a preparation for a film review (homework, Copymaster 19, p. 54).

6.6 Quotes and scenes from *The Giver* for further discussion

Copymaster 20, p. 55

Copymaster 20 provides a list of quotes. The students are to identify the context from which the quotes are taken and then discuss them further. This can also make for suitable tasks in oral exams (tandem exams). In this case, you might want to come up with a few prompting questions, depending on your students' proficiency.

The quotes are taken from:
Quote 1: (**79** 16–18)
Quote 3: (**83** 33–36)
Quote 5: (**84** 6–20)
Quote 6: (**100** 4–16; cf. Orwell, Newspeak, available as download)
Quote 4 (**103** 3–6, 20-22)
Quote 2: (**111** 22–25)

7. Test papers

Students tend to learn most in and from their own test papers because they take this writing most seriously. The writing assignments in such a situation should refer back to what the students have learned so far, so that they can prepare for the test. In addition, the assignments should be challenging to young people's minds; they should be interesting to write about. For this reason the students are offered a selection of four assignments so that they can choose a topic that they feel comfortable with. The students should also be reminded to focus their attention on the essay form. Adding a few hints as to the organization of the paper will certainly make for better results.

Copymaster 21, p. 56

The two tasks are presented on Copymaster 21, p. 56.

Time allowance: 2 lessons.

Possible solution:

Task 1: Jonas' diary entry written after he has reached Elsewhere

Entries should contain:

- Jonas' excitement/apprehension before the selection,
- his strange "job",

- his meeting with the Giver,
- the joy and pain he experienced,
- the twin's release as an eye-opener that triggered his decision to abduct Gabriel and escape;
- his stressful journey to Elsewhere,
- the snow and the sled,
- the house in Elsewhere;
- the strange songs,
- the joy of snow, mountains, colors,
- the dangers in the new society,
- the difficulty to find a place to stay, a permanent job, an education,
- the danger of wars, storms…,
- what to do with Gabe,
- the worries about his sister, his friends, the Giver …

Task 2: Relating a picture to the novel:

Possible solution:
The description of the picture should focus on the metaphorical depiction of the loudspeaker (seeing and hearing everything, controlling people's lives, some people cheering, agreeing with everything, others thoughtful. The loudspeaker stands for total control of people's activities.

For the application of the picture to *The Giver*, different answers are imaginable, because the people depicted have different reactions to total control:

positive: happiness, no worries, carefree life; or:

negative: no freedom , fitting with major rules, living a life that is regulated by others…, fear of feelings, memories coming back…

This is a very open task. Students might well have ideas that cannot be anticipated here.

8. Worksheets / Copymasters

Role cards

JONAS, age 11, lives with his father, mother and sister in a house given to them by the Community. He likes cycling. One day, while riding along the river, he remembers when, about a year before, he saw an unidentified plane passing over the community. He is still frightened by this; perhaps the pilot had made a mistake and had been "released". He is also frightened by the future: soon, in December, there will be the "Ceremony of Twelve". He is choosing his words carefully and wonders if the word "frightened" is the right word for both experiences.

LILY, age 7, is Jonas' sister. She likes to talk. One evening in the "telling of feelings" at home, she complains about a group visiting her childcare group of Sevens who did not obey the rules. It made her angry and she compares them to "animals"; a word which is used to describe uneducated people who do not respect the rules of the community. After her father and Jonas have told her that the visitors might just have felt sad because they are from a different community with different rules, she apologizes for her intolerance and ignorance.

FATHER, a "nurturer", is responsible for the physical and emotional development of newborn babies, called "newchildren". He is sad and worried about one baby who is not doing well, who does not sleep soundly and isn't growing as fast as he should be. Therefore, it might soon be "released". Father thinks about taking the baby home at night because the night crew of nurturers are not taking care of him well enough.

MOTHER holds an important position at the Department of Justice. She is in charge of punishing offenders. She is frustrated and feels guilty when a criminal is brought to court a second time. She is frightened because after three trials, an offender is usually "released".

ASHER, age 11, is Jonas' best friend. He is not careful about his language, talks too fast and sometimes mixes up words, which often has a comical effect. He gets distracted easily and has to apologize to his "learning community" afterwards, e.g. when he is late for school.

NEWCHILD (is only talked about, makes no physical appearance in the chapter) is a sweet, very young baby boy who does not sleep very well and does not grow as fast as he should. Although he is of a lovely disposition, he is a problem child and is kept in the extra care section for supplementary (extra) nurturing. Might be "released" (set free?, let go?).

ISBN 978-3-12-578137-5

The Community

Read Chapter 2. What do you find out about the Community ?
Complete the table below.

Family units	
Rules	
Ceremony (of Twelve)	
The Elders	
The Receiver	
Assignments / Training	
School / Play / Volunteer work	

ISBN 978-3-12-578137-5

Reading Tasks

While reading the book, each of you will concentrate on one of the themes/questions below. Please read closely and take notes.

Themes/Tasks	Students' name
The Community	
What rules and regulations exist and to what extent do they have to be obeyed?	
What ceremonies are there and what purpose do they have?	
How and when do children develop independence?	
What does the Community look and sound like? (landscape / architecture / traffic / technology)	
What is the relationship between the authorities and the citizens?	
Other communities and the outside world – "Elsewhere"	
How do other communities differ?	
Where is "Elsewhere" and what is said about it?	
Individual characters: outward appearance and personality	
Jonas	
Gabe	
Lily	
Mother	
Father	
The Giver	
Asher	
Other characters	
Language	
Release	
Dramatizing scenes through screenplays	
Vocabulary notebook organized in semantic maps etc.	
Reading journal	

ISBN 978-3-12-578137-5

Klett

Word list

The following word list contains the key words from The Giver which you will need when talking or writing about the novel or film. The words marked with an asterisk (*) were created by the author and have a meaning very specific to the novel. Worksheet 5 outlines some strategies on how to memorize these words.
*The numbers indicate the word's first occurrence in the text. The first number (in bold), is the page number; the second number indicates the line on that page. So **25** 2 means the word first occurs on page 25, line 2.*

- ☐ announcement **25** 2
- ☐ anthem **10** 34
- ☐ to apologize for **10** 23
- ☐ appeal **20** 10
- ☐ to apply for **31** 15
- ☐ appropriate **15** 16
- ☐ assembly **17** 17
- ☐ to assign **14** 17
- ☐ awe **15** 24
- ☐ birthmother **23** 19
- ☐ brave **54** 4
- ☐ burden **85** 9
- ☐ capacity **14** 20
- ☐ celebration **14** 6
- ☐ ceremony **15** 21
- ☐ to chant **10** 34
- ☐ chastisement **23** 15
- ☐ chief **45** 8
- ☐ choice **28** 11
- ☐ citizen **9** 21
- ☐ collective **52** 2
- ☐ command **36** 18
- ☐ committee **13** 34
- ☐ community **9** 5
- ☐ to complain **14** 16
- ☐ to contribute **5** 10
- ☐ (in)convenient **126** 26
- ☐ to correspond **44** 12
- ☐ counsel **83** 27
- ☐ crew **9** 29
- ☐ decision **10** 15
- ☐ destruction **90** 19
- ☐ discipline **47** 19
- ☐ disgrace **13** 5
- ☐ elderly **12** 6
- ☐ to elect **46** 6
- ☐ (un)endurable **88** 16
- ☐ event **9** 20
- ☐ exhausting **40** 23
- ☐ failure **10** 16
- ☐ family unit* **14** 21
- ☐ honor **24** 11
- ☐ humiliation **25** 12
- ☐ instructor **9** 5
- ☐ interdependence **38** 20
- ☐ major **34** 19
- ☐ match **10** 20
- ☐ mate **80** 6
- ☐ memory **52** 5
- ☐ minor **29** 1
- ☐ mischief **45** 8
- ☐ misbehavior **45** 7
- ☐ to modify **52** 35
- ☐ newchild* **13** 25
- ☐ nourishment **47** 6
- ☐ nurturer* **13** 26
- ☐ to obey **12** 16
- ☐ observation **19** 12
- ☐ obsolete **69** 32
- ☐ order **9** 15
- ☐ pain **48** 18
- ☐ to perceive **67** 32
- ☐ placement **39** 28
- ☐ (un)predictable **69** 30
- ☐ protective **38** 24
- ☐ public **11** 2
- ☐ punishment **10** 15
- ☐ to receive **16** 8
- ☐ recreation **19** 14
- ☐ to release* **10** 11
- ☐ reminder **25** 5
- ☐ replacement **41** 1
- ☐ request **108** 11
- ☐ resignation **134** 30
- ☐ ritual **12** 3
- ☐ rude **23** 12
- ☐ rule **9** 11
- ☐ sameness* **69** 32
- ☐ selection **18** 30
- ☐ solemn **27** 11
- ☐ spouse **14** 19
- ☐ to standardize **46** 14
- ☐ stir **27** 5
- ☐ successor **10** 8
- ☐ to suffer **84** 15
- ☐ training **10** 8
- ☐ transgression **15** 2
- ☐ to transmit **64** 26
- ☐ violation **42** 22
- ☐ volunteer **19** 10
- ☐ wand* **48** 17
- ☐ watchful **41** 3

ISBN 978-3-12-578137-5

Vocabulary – Learning strategies

There are many strategies for learning vocabulary. Here are four suggestions to help you memorize the key words from the word list. Knowing them will help you to speak and write about The Giver.

Strategy 1: Categorize words

Put as many words as you can into the categories below. Not all of them fit.

Community	Citizens	The Giver	Jonas	Families
	manage	failure burden	in awe brave carry the burden	adequate appropriate birthmother family unit

Strategy 2: Mind maps

If you are a more visual learner, then maybe arranging words in a mind map will help you to memorize them. For example, if you choose 'Committee of Elders' as your headword, your mind map might look like this:

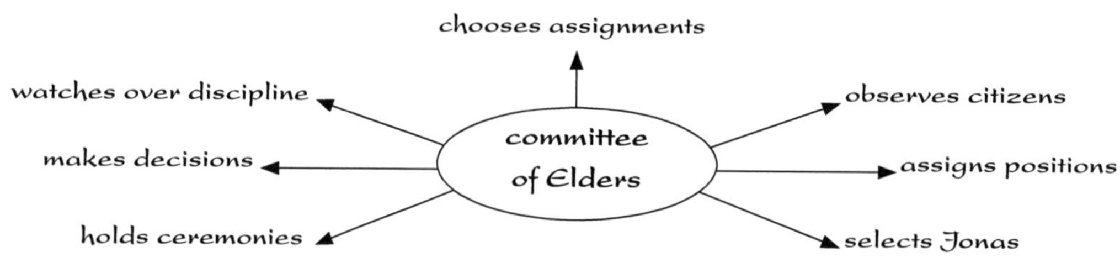

Strategy 3: Tick words you have used

While you are working on any assignment related to *The Giver,* tick any words you have used on the list. Try to use as many as possible. Once you have used the words yourself, you will find that they are easier to remember.

Strategy 4: Expand the list

If you are keeping a vocabulary notebook, you could expand the list, by adding an example sentence, synonyms (words with the same or similar meaning) and antonyms (words with the opposite meaning), translations, collocations etc. For example:

Key word	Example sentence	Translation	Word family	synonym/antonym
to assign	The jobs were assigned to the Twelves in a ceremony.	zuteilen	assignment (Aufgabe)	to allocate

ISBN 978-3-12-578137-5

How to keep a good reading journal

Here are a few ideas for your reading journal. Tick the ones you have used or intend to use:

- ☐ summarize the book as you go along and write personal responses to certain parts: spontaneous reactions, questions, predictions (ideas on how the book might go on), etc.
- ☐ add material from newspapers, magazines, encyclopedias, the internet and other sources on related topics or similar literary works, the author, her works, etc.
- ☐ write the journal as a diary from a character's point of view (use hints from the text and your own imagination)
- ☐ quote your favorite passages from the book and explain why you like them
- ☐ add vocabulary that is interesting, typical and necessary to describe certain facts, events or characters
- ☐ create dialogues from narrated parts
- ☐ write a script for a play or a film
- ☐ collect the vocabulary in word fields (you may get together with a partner who specializes in another word field and later put everything together)
- ☐ select music that might fit the atmosphere of the novel
- ☐ make a list of film titles that deal with the same or a similar topic
- ☐ find suitable poetry
- ☐ write your own poetry
- ☐ rewrite parts that you don't like (e.g. the beginning or ending) or that you want to expand on
- ☐ draw pictures or find photos of paintings, sculptures and/or other photos
- ☐ design a new book cover
- ☐ write a book review for other students and look at other people's reviews (for example at amazon.com or goodreads.com)

ISBN 978-3-12-578137-5

Chapter 5: Jonas' First Stirrings
Setting: The Family's Dream-telling Ritual in the Morning
Characters: Mother, Father, Jonas, Lily
It is Dream-telling time. The family is sitting at the breakfast table.

MOTHER: Jonas, it's your turn.

JONAS *(shifting in his chair)*: I did dream last night.

FATHER: Good, Jonas, tell us.

JONAS: The details aren't clear, I think I was in the bathing room at the House of the Old.

FATHER: That's where you were yesterday.

JONAS *(nodding)*: But, it wasn't really the same. There was a tub in the dream, but only one. And a real bathing room has rows and rows of them. But the room in the dream was warm and damp. And I had taken off my tunic, but hadn't put on the smock, so my chest was bare. I was perspiring because it was so warm. And Fiona was there, the way she was yesterday.

MOTHER: Asher too?

JONAS *(shaking his head)*: It was only me and Fiona, alone in the room standing beside the tub. She was laughing, but I wasn't. I was almost a little angry at her in the dream because she wasn't taking me seriously.

LILY: Seriously? About what?

JONAS *(uneasy)*: I think I was trying to convince her that she should get into the tub of water. I wanted her to take off her clothes and get into the tub of water. I wanted to bathe her. I had the sponge in my hand. But she wouldn't. She was laughing and kept saying "no". *(Looking at his parents)* That's all.

FATHER: Can you describe the strongest feeling in your dream, son?

JONAS: The wanting. I knew that she wouldn't. And I think I knew that she shouldn't. But I wanted it so terribly. I could feel the wanting all through me.

MOTHER *(uneasy)*: Thank you for your dream, Jonas.

Father and Lily get up. Jonas, still in thought, gets up as well.

MOTHER: Jonas, wait.

Jonas sinks back down into his chair, watching his mother tidying the remains of the morning meals. Then she sits down next to him.

MOTHER: Jonas, the feeling you described as the wanting? It was your first Stirrings. Father and I have been expecting it to happen to you for a long time. It happens to everyone. It happened to Father when he was your age. And it happened to me. Someday it will happen to Lily. And very often, it begins with a dream.

JONAS: Do I have to report it?

MOTHER: You did, in the dream-telling. That's enough.

JONAS: But what about the treatment? The speaker always reminds us that treatment must take place.

MOTHER: No, no. It's just the pills. You're ready for the pills. That's all. That's the treatment for the Stirrings. *(She goes and gets the pills.)* Here you are, Jonas. But don't forget. From now on you have to take them regularly. One every day, every day of your life until you go to the House of the Old. All of your adult life. But it becomes routine; after a while you won't even pay much attention to it.

ISBN 978-3-12-578137-5

Infosheet for scriptwriters

When writing your script, try to come up with three Acts. Keep in mind the dramatic tension and plot points as illustrated below.

Act I
Setup:
The community is introduced

Act II
Confrontation:
Jonas learns about the memories that he has to carry for the whole community

Act III
Resolution:
Jonas escapes (and reaches Elsewhere)

Plot Point I
Jonas receives his assignment

Plot Point II
Jonas witnesses the release of the twin and plans his escape

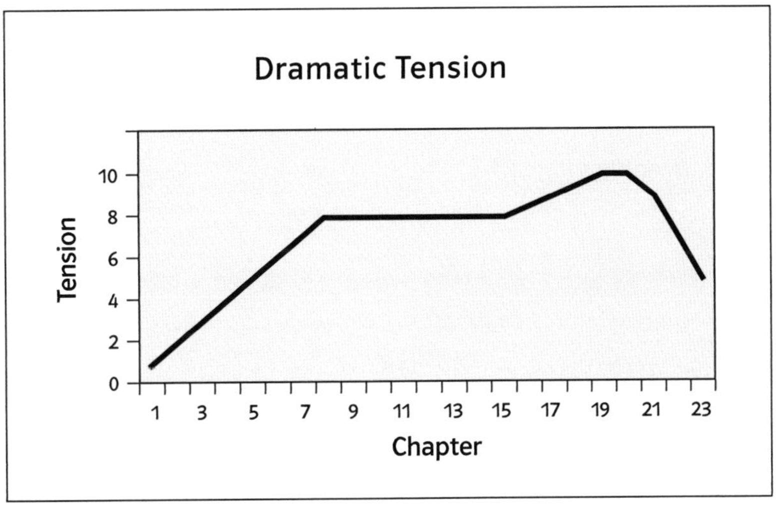

ISBN 978-3-12-578137-5

Chapters 7–8: The Ceremony of Twelve

Characters: Chief Elder, Jonas, Narrator, Giver, Audience/Community

NARRATOR: It was a long session. All of the Twelves have been assigned their life-time jobs; Inger was assigned birthmother, Isaac became a teacher of Sixes, only Jonas was not assigned a job.

CHIEF ELDER: I know you are all concerned. You think I have made a mistake and left out Jonas.
I caused you anxiety. I apologize to my Community.

THE COMMUNITY: We accept your apology.

CHIEF ELDER: Jonas, I especially apologize to you. I have caused you anguish.

JONAS: I accept your apology.

CHIEF ELDER: Please come up to the stage now.

THE COMMUNITY: *(murmuring)* What does this mean?

CHIEF ELDER: Jonas has not been assigned, Jonas has been selected. He has been selected to be our next Receiver of Memory. Such a selection is very, very rare. Our Community only has one Receiver.

JONAS: Receiver of Memory?

CHIEF ELDER: We have observed Jonas very carefully in the past and found that he is worth being selected. He is intelligent and wise and above all, he has the Capacity to See Beyond.

JONAS: *(blinking, showing his astonishment)*
No, I… No, I….
(His face clears up.)
But yes, yes … I think it's true. I don't know what it is. But sometimes I see something. And maybe it is beyond.

CHIEF ELDER: *(speaking to the entire community)*
Jonas, you will be trained to be our next Receiver of Memory. We thank you for your childhood.

THE COMMUNITY: (the murmuring becoming louder and louder):
Jonas, Jonas, Jonas … *(seven times)*

ISBN 978-3-12-578137-5

Talking about Jonas' rules

In Chapter 9, Jonas receives the rules and instructions for his training as Receiver of Memory. How does he react? Complete the table and support your ideas with evidence from the text.

Chapter 9: **Rules for the new Receiver**	**Jonas' reactions (p. 58–60)**
Go to your training immediately after school every day.	
Go home immediately after your training.	
You may be rude: i.e. ask any citizen any question and you will receive answers.	
Don't discuss your training with anybody, not even parents and Elders.	
You must not tell anyone about your dreams any more.	
Except for illness and injury that has nothing to do with your training you must not ask for medicine.	
You may not apply for release.	
You may lie.	

ISBN 978-3-12-578137-5

How does Jonas react to the memories that the Giver transmits to him? What is said about these memories? Take notes while reading Chapters 10–18.

Memory	Impact on Jonas	Why abolished? / Comments
snow (hill) **sunshine** **sunburn**		
color		
animals (elephants)		
bone fracture; pain		
colorful memories of nature		
suffering of the past: destruction, **hunger,** **warfare**		
love: families, holidays, happiness		

ISBN 978-3-12-578137-5

Infosheet: Writing I

Comparing and contrasting:
When you compare and contrast people, events, etc., make use of connective expressions. For example:

Phrase	Example
on the one hand … on the other hand	**On the one hand**, Jonas could not apply for release, **on the other hand** he did not consider it anyway.
however, yet	Jonas, **however**, could not apply for release.
whereas, while	Rosemary could apply for release, **whereas** Jonas could not.
unlike, in contrast to	**Unlike (in contrast to)** Rosemary, Jonas could not apply for release.
comparing … with, when I compare	**Comparing** Jonas **with** Rosemary, I can say…
to be different from … in that	Jonas **is different from** Rosemary **in that**…
to differ from	He **differs from** Rosemary.
to be similar to sb in that; to behave in a similar way	Jonas **behaves in a similar way as** Rosemary when he …
similarity, difference	There are **similarities (differences)** in their attitudes.

Describing people, objects, concepts, situations:

When asked to describe something, try to follow these useful suggestions:

1. Use connectives like:
   at first, then, after that, while, after, at the same time, simultaneously
2. Try to vary your style by using gerunds and participles.
3. Make use of synonyms to avoid repetition:
   Jonas witnesses the release of a twin. He ***sees (watches / observes)*** *his father open the cupboard and …*
4. When talking about feelings, the following expressions can be useful:
   At first he is curious, interested, then he is surprised, stunned, shocked, in a state of shock, grieved, utterly sad, depressed, downcast, heavy-hearted, devastated; he feels a choking sensation, pain.

Useful phrases to describe an area / a landscape / community (town, city):

- it is surrounded **by** …
- it is located **on/near** …
- it has a population **of** …
- the population **consists of** …
- largely/to a great extent …
- many years ago it turned **to** … and developed **into** …
- inhabitants work/are employed **in** …
- the community is separated **from** … **by**

ISBN 978-3-12-578137-5

Infosheet: Writing II

Basic rules for writing summaries

→ **Begin with an introductory sentence:**	*The last four chapters deal with / focus on …*
→ **Summarize facts only:**	*It begins and ends with …* *At first…, then…, after that …*
→ **Use the present tense:**	*He tries to … –* ***not:*** *He tried to …*
→ **Use factual, not descriptive or narrative language:**	Feelings are also facts, but just state how someone feels, don't describe the feeling in detail.
→ **Don't describe details:**	i.e. the color of sb's shoes or the style of sb's clothes are not important in a summary
→ **Combine sentences by using subordinate clauses:**	*When he escapes for the first time, he is caught by …*

How to tell a story:

When narrating a story, in contrast when writing summaries, you should make readers feel the situation / experience the events as if they themselves were involved in the action.
For connectives see Copymaster 12.
→ Be descriptive.
→ Use direct speech.
→ Use concrete rather than abstract words.

Synonyms

You can avoid repetition and make your text sound more interesting by using synonyms. You can look these up in a monolingual dictionary or a thesaurus. If you are typing your text on the computer, you can access the thesaurus directly from MS Word for example (hit 'Shift' + F7).

In a text on how the Community in *The Giver* is regulated, you would expect words like *allow, forbid* and *force*. Look at the following table and see if you can improve your text by using some of the synonyms presented.

to allow	to forbid	to force
• People are **allowed to** … • Riding bicycles is **not allowed** before … • They are **permitted** to … • They are **given permission** to … • An assignment **may** be appealed against.	• It is **forbidden** for people to … • … is **strictly forbidden** • Reading for pleasure is **prohibited** by rule • Citizens are **denied the right** to … • Books are **banned from** … • A **ban is imposed on** …	• They are **forced to** … • The authorities **make them** obey the rules by … • They **put pressure on them** to … • They **pressure sb into** doing sth.

ISBN 978-3-12-578137-5

Creative writing: Writing a poem

1. Write ten words or phrases from the book that come to your mind (in 60 seconds) underneath each other in the middle of a page:

Example:

Gabe
problem
child
nurturer
care
crib
escape
elsewhere
what if
die

2. Then connect these words with each other by completing the lines. It is not necessary for your poem to rhyme.

Sample poem:

Who is Gabe?
A problem
child?
A nurturer's case?
Who cares for him
crying and fretting in his crib?
Is escape to
Elsewhere a solution?
What if
he dies, even there?

ISBN 978-3-12-578137-5

Summary of reading tasks

You and a partner will now swap your findings on the reading tasks you chose at the beginning of the unit. Take notes.

Themes	Findings
The community	Population: Citizens: Recreation and play: School and training: People's looks: Rules and regulations: Relationship between authorities and citizens: Housing: Government: History: Work:
Ceremonies	
Landscape: Architecture: Sounds: Color: Traffic: Technology:	
Other communities and the outside world – Elsewhere	
Characters	Jonas: Gabriel: Lily: Mother: Father: The Giver: Rosemary: Asher: Fiona:
Language	
Release	

ISBN 978-3-12-578137-5

Panel discussion

You are going to have a panel discussion on the advantages and disadvantages of the society presented in *The Giver.*

- Choose from one of the scenarios below or come up with your own scenario.
- Assign roles (ideally two students per role, so you can help each other out).
- Prepare your arguments.
- Get started.

Scenario 1:
The Giver, Jonas and Rosemary meet with the Chief Elder, a Birthmother, Asher, Father or other characters from the book and try to persuade them to change their society.
Roles required: Host, Giver, Jonas, Rosemary, Chief Elder, Birthmother, Asher, Father, …

Scenario 2:
The Giver, Jonas and Rosemary meet with representatives of our own contemporary society (e.g. a volunteer who works in the Developing World, a conservative or a socialist politician, a nurse, a social worker), who see serious problems in our society and who advise them to go back to the Community.
Roles required: Host, Giver, Jonas, Rosemary, volunteer, conservative politician, socialist politician, nurse, social worker, …

Depending on the scenario you have chosen, prepare your role for the panel discussion. The following phrases will help you:

agreeing, disagreeing, discussing

- I agree with …
- I share your/his/her opinion.
- I don't agree. / I disagree.
- I don't think so. / I don't think this is true.
- It's a mistake to think that …
- I'm against the idea of… / I object to the idea …
- I am of a totally different opinion.

ISBN 978-3-12-578137-5

Sample reviews

☆☆☆☆☆ **A Great Futuristic Book**

I really like this book because it makes you think about what life could be like if everything was the same. The story is about Jonas, a boy who lives in a community where there is a condition called "Sameness". Sameness is when all people are the same. No color is seen. There is a rule for everything. When Jonas is selected as Receiver of Memory, an honored position of the only person who has memories of what life used to be like, he learns of all the things that used to occur and do not anymore. He is unhappy, and wants to get out of Sameness and into "Elsewhere". Lois Lowry has such a great writing style and I love to read her books. She is so descriptive and she makes you feel like you're there, living the story with Jonas. I recommend this book to anyone.

☆☆☆☆☆ **Once you've started this, you can't put it down until the end**

The Giver by Lois Lowry concerns a teenage boy growing up in a society where all emotions are repressed, births are strictly controlled and those who don't fit in are "released". I won't say too much about it, because there are a couple of plot features which I could spoil. What I will say is that it is brilliantly written – the reader can instantly empathize with the central character – incredibly moving and altogether believable. (N.B. This is a young adults' title, but don't let that put any adult readers off.)

☆☆☆☆☆ **I did NOT like this book.**

I have enjoyed previous books by this author, but this one I did not like. Rarely do I dislike a book, but this is at the top of my not like list. I will say that it is powerful and thought-provoking reading, but I felt my soul, my being, was being ripped apart, and all that I have believed and hoped was being questioned.

ISBN 978-3-12-578137-5
Klett

You are going to watch the film The Giver *and compare it to the novel. While or after watching the film take notes on differences. Keep in mind the points you focussed on for your reading task.*

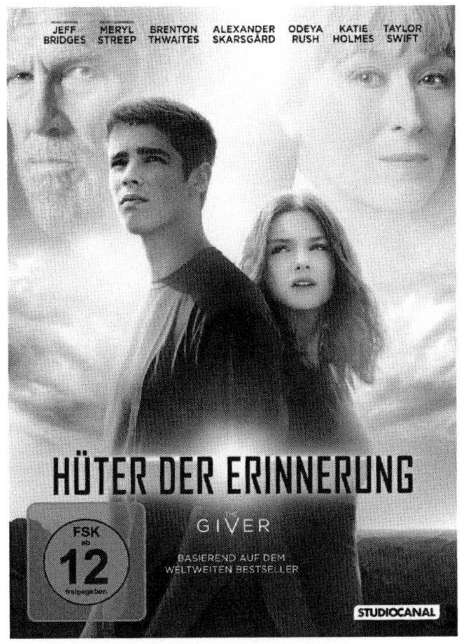

What does the Community look like? (architecture, landscape, border traffic, loudspeakers, etc.)

-
-
-

How do people behave?

What do the characters look like? (clothes, hairstyles, make-up ...)

-
-
-

The Ending

What do you dislike?

What has been added, what left out?

What could have been omitted?

What would you have done differently?

What do you like?

ISBN 978-3-12-578137-5

Writing a film review

Remember: The purpose of a **film review** is to inform readers about it and to either recommend it or to warn people against it.

Write a review for a young people's magazine.

Inform your readers about:

- some of the plot (not all of it);
- suspense, credibility, similarities and differences between novel and movie;
- maybe what's missing in the movie in contrast to the book or vice versa;
- the characters and actors;
- the setting.

At one point, maybe at the end, there should be a clear recommendation or a warning.
Rate the film by using stars (1 being worst and 5 being best) *****

The following excerpt is the beginning of a film review by David Edwards. You can either finish writing this one, or complete your own.
Don't plagiarize (i.e. copy what other people have written)!

Movie Review: *The Giver* (12A) 97mins by David Edwards (Daily Record, September 19, 2014)

The Giver

**** Young adults impatient for the next instalment of *The Hunger Games* will find plenty to enjoy in this thriller based on the Lois Lowry novel.

In the near future, following the unexplained "Ruin", society has been organised into communities where memories have been erased and emotions are banned.

It's against this dystopian backdrop that we meet the teenage Jonas (Brenton Thwaites), who's been chosen to be the receiver of past memories from The Giver (Jeff Bridges). As he learns of life in the past, Jonas develops …

ISBN 978-3-12-578137-5

Quotes for discussion

Identify the context in which the following quotes occur and discuss them.

Quote 1: "If everything's the same, then there aren't any choices! I want to wake up in the morning and decide things. A blue tunic or a red one?"

Quote 2: "You just stay away from the river, my friend […]. The community lost Rosemary after five weeks and it was a disaster for them. I don't know what the community would do if they lost you."

Quote 3: "Sometimes I wish they'd ask for my wisdom more often – there are so many things I could tell them; things I wish they would change. But they don't want change. Life here is so orderly, so predictable – so painless. It's what they've chosen."

Quote 4: Jonas realized that it was a new depth of feelings that he was experiencing. Somehow they were not at all the same as the feelings that every evening, in every dwelling, every citizen analyzed with endless talk. […]
But now Jonas had experienced real sadness. He had felt grief. He knew that there was no quick comfort for emotions like those. These were deeper and did not need to be told. They were felt.

Quote 5: The Giver smiled grimly. "When the new Receiver failed, the memories that she had received were released. They didn't come back to me. They went…"
He paused, and seemed to be struggling with the concept. "I don't know, exactly. They went to a place where memories once existed before Receivers were created. Someplace out there –" He gestured vaguely with his arm. "And then the people had access to them. Apparently that's the way it was, once. Everyone had access to memories. "It was chaos," he said. "They really suffered for a while. Finally it subsided as the memories were assimilated. But it certainly made them aware of how they need a Receiver to contain all that pain. And knowledge."
"But you have to suffer like that all the time," Jonas pointed out. The Giver nodded. "And you will. It's my life. It will be yours."

Quote 6: "Do you love me?"
There was an awkward silence for a moment. Then Father gave a little chuckle.
"Jonas. You of all people. Precision of language, please!"
"What do you mean?" Jonas asked. Amusement was not at all what he had anticipated.
"Your father means that you used a very generalized word, so meaningless that it's become almost obsolete," his mother explained carefully.
Jonas stared at them. Meaningless? He had never before felt anything as meaningful as the memory.
"And of course our community can't function smoothly if people don't use precise language."

ISBN 978-3-12-578137-5

Exam *The Giver*

Name: ______________________________

*Choose **one** of the following topics and use as much information as possible from the book.*

1. The diary entry Jonas wrote after he reached Elsewhere

Suppose Jonas has finally managed to escape. He has found a place to stay for Gabriel and himself. He is slowly getting used to his new surroundings and writes an entry in his diary, in which he thinks back to the time when he:

- was selected;
- received the memories;
- watched the twin's release;
- made the decision to escape.

He also notes down his experiences of his new life:

- what is strange to him;
- his worries about people (family, friends) he left;
- the dangers that are waiting for him and Gabe;
- his own new challenges.

You can choose the order in which you present your ideas. Start new paragraphs for new ideas. (A paragraph usually consists of more than one sentence.)

2. Relating a picture to the novel

Describe the picture and analyze its relationship to *The Giver.*
Jot down a few notes and make an outline.
Then write an introduction (first paragraph).
For each new point/idea, start a new paragraph. (A paragraph usually consists of more than one sentence.)
Sometimes transitions from one paragraph to the next *(although, in spite of; because, as, because of, due to …)* make for good reading.
A last paragraph should sum up your ideas nicely.

A note on the picture:
The picture was inspired by Bernhard Heisig's painting *Gewieher* (1995). In the original, horse heads are attached to each side of the loudspeaker, which have been removed. The original painting reflects Heisig's preoccupation with totalitarian regimes. Bernhard Heisig lived from 1928 until 2011 and spent all his life in Eastern Germany (mostly Leipzig).

ISBN 978-3-12-578137-5

III Teaching the film *The Giver*

1. The film

1.1 Bibliographical information

Film: The Giver *(Hüter der Erinnerung)*
Director: Philip Noyce *(Riot Games, Clear and Present Danger, The Bone Collector, Rabbit Proof Fence, The Quiet American, Salt)*
Screenwriters: Michael Mitnick and Robert B. Weide
Main actors: Brenton Thwaites (Jonas), Odeya Rush (Fiona), Cameron Monaghan (Asher), Meryl Streep (Chief Elder), Jeff Bridges (The Giver), Alexander Skarsgård (father), Katie Holmes (mother)
Director of Photography: Ross Emery *(The Matrix, Superman Returns)*
Producer: Nikki Silver, Jeff Bridges, Neil Koenigsberg
Weinstein Company and Walden Media, 2014
In Germany: Studiocanal, 2015 (Languages: German & English, Subtitles: German only)
Running time: 93 minutes
Note: The STUDIOCANAL version distributed in Germany only has German subtitles. If you want English subtitles, you should order the film from a British company.

1.2 Chapter Overview

Chapter	Summary	Time
Chapter 1	Introduction to: the protagonists, the Community and its rules, the ceremony.	0:00:40 – 0:12:25
Chapter 2	The training as Receiver begins; Jonas receives the first memories.	0:12:28 – 0:21:27
Chapter 3	Jonas starts to change and acts against the rules. The Chief Elder becomes suspicious.	0:21:30 – 0:31:00
Chapter 4	Jonas receives more memories of the past.	0:31:01 – 0:40:00
Chapter 5	Jonas manages to calm Gabe and dreams of Fiona.	0:40:04 – 0:49:40
Chapter 6	Jonas gets to know Rosemary, the previous Receiver. He sees his father release a twin.	0:49:50 – 0:59:00
Chapter 7	Jonas decides to leave and take Gabe with him.	0:59:05 – 1:07:30
Chapter 8	The Chief Elder visits the Giver and arrests him. Asher pursues and catches Jonas and Gabe, and then drops them into a river.	1:07:34 – 1:17:48
Chapter 9	The Giver and the Chief Elder argue about the "achievements" of the Community. Jonas and Gabe arrive in Elsewhere.	1:17:50 – 1: 24:49
Chapters 10 & 11	Credits	1:24:50 – 1:34:16

1.3 Scene sequence

Time	Setting	Plot	Quotations
Chapter 1			
0:00:40	The Community from above	Trailer: The Community and its rules are introduced.	*From the ashes of The Ruin the Communities were built.* *Protected by the boundary.* *All memories of the past were erased.*
0:01:35	The Community: outside	Jonas introduces himself while riding his bike. He describes the Community and the future assignments; then he meets Asher and Fiona.	"Tomorrow we'd be assigned our jobs." "I always felt like I saw things differently." "I didn't want to be different. Who would?" "We lived in a world where differences were not allowed. [...] Our elders had eliminated all of that so there'd be no conflict between us."
0:03:30	At the nurturing center	The three friends hear a baby boy crying; Fiona is able to calm him down. They hear Jonas' father calling the baby by its name: Gabriel (even though at this stage, names are against the rules).	Father: "The little guy didn't qualify for tomorrow's ceremony."
0:04:55	Outside near the fountain	The three friends talk about friendship: they vow to be friends forever.	Asher:" Who are we?" Fiona: "Friends. Friends forever!"
0:06:00	At Jonas' "dwelling"	The family unit talks about "release" and feelings and Jonas' future assignment.	Jonas: "I'm sort of terrified." Mother: "Precision of language." Jonas: "I mean 'anxious'."
0:06: 53 – 0:11:28	In the Auditorium	The ceremony	*Ceremony of the release to Elsewhere.* *'Joyous retirement' to Elsewhere.* "All of your training has been to help you fit in." "Today, we honor your differences."
Chapter 2			
0:11:50	At Jonas' "dwelling"	Jonas receives the rules regarding his future assignment.	"From this moment, you are exempt from all rules governing rudeness."
0:14:15	Near the edge	Jonas cycles to the edge.	"I'd have to get close to it [the edge] every day for the rest of my life."

Time	Setting	Plot	Quotations
0:14:25	At the Giver's house	Jonas receives his first memories of the past: of snow, home (not dwelling), Christmas. He realizes that he also receives the names of unknown items (snow, sled).	"They're called books." "You will learn the secret history of the world." "There is no snow because of climate control."
0:20:30	Outside, Community grounds	Jonas and the Giver go for a walk and talk about lying and about the last Receiver before Jonas. The Receiver calls himself the Giver.	Jonas: "If I'm the new Receiver what does that make you?" Receiver: "Well, that must make me the Giver."
Chapter 3			
0:21:40	At Jonas' "dwelling"	Jonas' mother thinks Jonas has changed. Gabe is brought to the house.	"We had the same mark." "I felt that one day Gabriel would be chosen, too."
0:23:10	At the Giver's house	Jonas receives more memories (pain, sailing, sunset, color). He sees red apples. Elsewhere is close enough to touch.	"Our people created sameness."
0:25:34	Under a tree near the triangle	Fiona finds Jonas under a tree. He tries to help her see color. Asher joins them. They see drones. They talk about Elsewhere, which Asher has seen from above.	"You're seeing something, aren't you?" "So many secrets."
0:28:10	On the roof of the government center / auditorium, sliding down the solar panels	Jonas and Fiona act against the rules by sliding down the solar panels attached to the auditorium on lunch trays and by holding hands.	*Citizens are reminded that it is impolite to touch Community members outside your family unit.*
0:30:00	At the Giver's house	The Chief Elder reminds the Giver of the rules; she is concerned about the Receiver (the Giver) becoming reckless. She reminds him of his previous failure.	"Don't fail us again."
Chapter 4			
0:31:04	At the Giver's house	The Giver and Jonas find a map of the Community and its outer edge, the boundary of memory. The Giver shows Jonas a piano and plays music while talking about emotions, i.e. very deep feelings, a concept that needs to be explained to Jonas.	"That boundary is meant to keep memories in." "There is also such a thing as hearing beyond." Giver: "Emotions." Jonas: "You mean like feelings?" Giver: "Feelings are just fleeting, on the surface. But emotions, they're very deep, primal, they linger."

Time	Setting	Plot	Quotations
0:34:30	At the Giver's house	More memories are transmitted: of a folklore wedding with dancing, kissing, merriment.	"Listen to what's calling from inside."
0:35:20	At Jonas' "dwelling"	Jonas dances with Lilly. The Chief Elder appears and expresses her concern about the Giver becoming irresponsible. Jonas tells her that the Giver and he only talk, all the time. Jonas calms Gabe; he kisses Fiona in his dream.	"Are you being properly prepared? What do you and the receiver actually do?"
0:37:20	At the Giver's house	Jonas receives many more memories of different cultures, animals, etc. He describes them and his feelings of confusion. The Giver supports Jonas in becoming more self-confident. Jonas receives his first negative memory (of an elephant being shot dead).	"I saw sights and sounds I had no words to describe … I didn't know what to think, what to believe."
Chapter 5			
0:40:04	At Jonas' "dwelling"	Jonas calms Gabe by telling him (and sharing a memory) about real animals. He watches Fiona combing her hair in the house opposite.	"This comfort object is not a hippo. It's an elephant, and once, it was real and it was beautiful."
0:42:00	Outside, on a walk with the Giver	Jonas and the Giver talk about his dream, his feelings and love.	"A dream. A combination of reality, fantasy, emotions and what you had for dinner."
0:43:06	Outside on a bike path	Fiona asks Jonas why he is behaving in an unusual manner.	"Why are you being weird?"
0:43:40	At Jonas' "dwelling"	Jonas asks his parents about love and tells Gabe that he loves him.	"Jonas used a word that is so antiquated it has no application today." "I love you, Gabriel."
0:45:00	At the Giver's house	Jonas receives more negative memories (war, death).	"I'm not strong enough." "This is what we need to know so we can advise."

Time	Setting	Plot	Quotations
0:47:00	Outside near the playground	Jonas ignores Asher and wishes to return to his childhood. Fiona feels that something is wrong. Jonas wants to quit his training. He asks Fiona to quit her injections by using an apple instead of her hand.	"The Elders erased war from our world." "Everything is wrong." "I thought about her now, all the time."
Chapter 6			
0:49:40 **0:52:18**	At the Giver's house	Jonas sees Rosemary, the previous Receiver, at the grand piano. The Giver tells Jonas that he gave her only good memories, but she asked for more. So he gave her the memory of a child removed from its mother. Rosemary couldn't stand it and asked to be released. The Giver makes Jonas watch that morning's release. Jonas finds out that Fiona will be trained to perform releases. Jonas becomes more and more critical of the Community.	"This is Rosemary, the previous Receiver. She no longer exists, except here and in my memories."
0:54:25	Outside, near the triangle	Jonas tells Fiona about love; they kiss. Jonas remembers his "stirrings" when he got his medication that stopped him from having any sexual feelings.	"Do you feel anything? Does it feel warm? Does it feel nice?" "Fiona, there is more, so much more."
0:56:20	At Jonas' "dwelling"	Jonas learns that Gabe will be released the following day. He prepares his escape and plans to take Gabe with him.	"They hadn't eliminated murder. They just called it by a different name."
0:58:00	Outside in front of the nurturing center	Asher tries to stop Jonas. Jonas punches him.	"It isn't my family."
Chapter 7			
0:59:00	At the Giver's house	Jonas tells the Giver that he must flee. The Giver informs Jonas that all the memories will return if he manages to cross the memory border. Therefore The Giver would stay behind to help the people deal with the resulting chaos.	"Something can be done. Gabe is in danger." "Something must be done." "If you had the map, why didn't you try to leave?" "I was waiting for someone like you."

Time	Setting	Plot	Quotations
1:00:38	At the government center and the Giver's house	The Chief Elder questions Jonas' mother about Jonas' behavior; she informs the Giver of Jonas' disappearance. Jonas decides that he is ready to leave. His training is accelerated. The Giver gives Jonas strength.	"He is lying." "I love you, Jonas." "You have the courage. Let me give you the strength."
1:02:30	Outside	The Chief Elder tells the Community police that Jonas is a rebel who must be stopped. With Fiona's help, Jonas steals Gabe. He promises to come back for Fiona. The Elders watch recordings of Jonas' transgressions. Jonas is pursued by the police.	Jonas: "Where is Gabe? Is he among these?" Fiona: "If he's back, then he'd be with our Uncertains."
Chapter 8			
1:07:30	Outside and beyond the edge	Jonas drives over the edge (the Community's boundary). The search is terminated while Jonas escapes into the desert. Fiona is arrested.	Subject lost to the edge. *Search terminated.*
1:07:31	At the Government Center	Asher tells an official about Jonas' escape. Fiona is given an injection.	"Friends forever, right?"
1:07:59	In the desert	Jonas is driving through the desert. He passes some memories of parental love on to Gabe to strengthen him.	"He told me I could draw strength from the memories. I knew by giving them to Gabe, I could protect him."
1:08:32	At the Government Center	The Chief Elder watches Jonas' escape and the recordings of his subversive interactions with Fiona.	"What has he taught you?"
1:08:55	At the Giver's house At the Government Center	The Chief Elder arrests The Giver. Fiona and The Giver are in prison. A Ceremony of Loss is celebrated for Jonas.	"We *will* find Jonas." "You must not say his name anymore."
1:10:35	At the Government Center Outside	The Chief Elder orders Asher to find and lose Jonas. Asher finds him and Gabe, sucks them on to the body of the drone, but then drops them into a river. He then tells the Chief Elder that he has completed his mission. Jonas and Gabe struggle through the desert.	"I want you to find him [Jonas]. And then, I want you to lose him." "Asher, if you are my friend, if you ever were my friend, can you please somehow trust me?" "I do trust you Jonas." "It was the memory of Fiona that kept me going."

Time	Setting	Plot	Quotations
1:15:15	In prison	Fiona is prepared for release by Jonas' mother. The Giver is listening.	"There will be a nice ceremony." "I felt things." "Something that's been stolen from me."
1:16:15	Outside the Community, somewhere in the mountains	Jonas is walking through deep snow.	"Please Gabe, tell her she should be here. Where is the tower, Gabe? The tower should be here."
Chapter 9			
1:17:48	In prison	Fiona is about to be released with the Committee of Elders (including the Giver) watching. The Chief Elder justifies their politics. The Giver argues against them.	"I'm not uncomfortable, I'm afraid." "Her name was Rosemary. She was my daughter. I loved her." "Do you know what that's like, to love someone?" People are weak; people are selfish.
1:20:15	In the mountains In the Government Center	Jonas finds a sled and sledges down the hill. The Giver tries to convince the Elders to stop Fiona's release. Jonas and Gabe pass the tower marking the Border of Memories and release the memories back to the Community. Alternating scenes of Jonas' sledge ride, released memories and Fiona's release ceremony.	"It is a sled." "We are living a life of shadows." "We must continue."
1:23:00	Back in the Community	The memories return to the Community. Fiona is saved. Jonas and Gabe arrive safely at the house from the first memory that the Giver had passed on to Jonas. Christmas is being celebrated inside.	I wish I had been there when the memories returned. I knew that Fiona was safe. The Giver had led us here.

2. Overview of the teaching unit

Lesson	Theme	Goals	Material
1	The three friends Jonas, Fiona, Asher – and a strange Community	**Content:** Getting to know the three friends who live in a strange society. **Language:** – Using the new vocabulary to describe the Community; – giving a characterization of the three friends; – making predictions (orally).	• Beginning of film (beginning – 0:03:19) • Board • Notebooks
2	The Community with its rules and regulations	**Content:** Learning about the Community and its rules and regulations. **Language:** – Improving viewing and listening comprehension competence; – note taking; – speaking about differences.	• Film: repetition of beginning combined with the ceremony scene (0:06:53 – 0:11:28). • Board • Notebooks
3	What does "love" mean?	**Content:** Getting to know that love is forbidden in the Community. **Language:** – Watching for important information; – reflecting and speaking about the absence of love and the absence of language to describe feelings.	• Film scene about Jonas' dream and love (0:41:00 – 0:45:00); • Worksheets 1–2, pp. 77–78: gapped screenplay
4 + 5	The real meaning of "release" and Jonas' decision to escape to Elsewhere	**Content:** Understanding that Jonas has to escape in order to save Gabriel. **Language:** – Viewing and listening comprehension; – using new words in context.	• Film scene of his father's release of the twin (0:52:15 – 1:00:00) • Worksheet 3, p. 79 (jumbled sentences)
6 + 7	The Giver and the Chief Elder argue about the Community	**Content:** Reflecting on and discussing the reason why the CommunityCommunity decided to bring about "sameness" in the new society. **Language:** – viewing and listening comprehension; matching characters and statements; writing and discussing (in roles) the pros and cons of the Community (repetition of vocabulary in context)	• Film scene in which the Giver and the Chief Elder discuss the Community (1:17:47 – 1:20:14) • Worksheet 4, p. 80 (who says what; sequence)
8	The ending	**Content:** Understanding the ending and critical discussion of it. **Language:** – viewing; – listening; – note taking; – discussing.	• Film scene in which Jonas finds the home (1:20:14 – end) • Worksheet 5, p. 81
9	Test	testing students' knowledge and critical evaluation	• Worksheet 6.1–6.3, pp. 82–84

3. Lesson plans

3.1 Lesson 1: The three friends Jonas, Fiona, Asher – and a strange Community

Goals:
- **Content:** Students get to know the three friends who live in a strange society.
- **Language:** With the help of the new vocabulary, students are able to describe the Community and give a general characterization of the three friends. They make oral predictions.

Material:
Film (beginning – 3:19)
Board
Notebooks

Activities:

Step 1: Key words from the scene are written on the board; students are asked to read words on the board. From these words students make predictions about what they are going to see.

Headline: "From the ashes of the Ruin the communities were built"
- rules
- boundary – border
- to erase memories – to wipe out (to eliminate) memories
- to obey the curfew *(Ausgangssperre beachten)*
- to assign *(vorschreiben)* clothing, jobs
- graduation ceremony – ceremony where jobs are assigned to young people
- to be scared
- to be different
- apology – excuse
- to apologize – to say sorry
- differences are not allowed
- to eliminate conflict: fear, pain, envy, hate

Step 2: Students watch the beginning of the film up to 3:19 twice; after/during the second viewing they take notes (some on transparencies) about what, who, where, when (how).

Step 3: If necessary, the excerpt is watched again to focus on differences in the Community: clothes, bikes, houses, language.

Step 4: Students predict who will be the protagonist and what the conflict might be.

Expected outcome
Step 2: After a comparison of students' notes a text like the following is written on the board:
A strange Community with strange rules is presented. Jonas (who does not have a last name) seems to be extraordinary. He sees things that other people don't. He doesn't want to be different. They live in a world where differences are not allowed. Feelings like fear, pain, envy and hate don't exist.

The three friends have been friends forever. Asher is funny: he makes everybody laugh. Fiona makes everyone smile.

Step 3: Similarities and differences between the Community and our society:

- clothes not different
- bikes all white, straight handlebars
- "dwellings" look like boxes, all alike
- language: the people say sorry all the time.

Jonas might be the protagonist because he says that he is different, but does not want to be different.

Step 4: Predictions

Students may predict that Jonas is the protagonist because he stands out. As differences are not allowed, conflicts might arise between him and his friends, or others.

3.2 Lesson 2: The Community with its rules and regulations

Material:

Film: beginning and the ceremony scene (0:06:53 – 0:11:28).

Board

Notebooks

Goals:

- **Content:** Students get to know the Community and its rules and regulations.
- **Language:** Improving viewing and listening comprehension competence combined with note taking competence. Speaking about differences.

Activities:

Step 1: **Headlines are written on the board**:

- Rules
- The Community
- The Ceremony
- Jonas' selection (word select – selection is explained)

Step 2: The beginning of the film including the Ceremony is watched. The scene with the Ceremony is watched twice (0:06:53 – 0:11:28).

Step 3: In pairs, students write as much as they can understand under the relevant heading during second viewing. (The film is stopped several times so that learners have time to write.)

Step 4: Notes are compared and written on the board. Things students have not understood are explained by the teacher.

Expected outcome written on the board:

Rules	The Community	The ceremony	Jonas' selection
In the Community there are many rules, for example: • Use precise language. • Wear assigned clothing. • Use your medication. • Obey the curfew. • Never lie. • People don't have last names; they are assigned jobs at a ceremony.	• In the Community there are no losers, no winners. • There are no feelings, either negative or positive. • People wear the same clothes. • There are no colors. • The Community is said to be a beautiful place where people live in harmony, not chaos. • People apologize all the time. They are very polite. • They applaud and chant in a chorus when Jonas is selected.	In the Ceremony several things are celebrated: • The elderly's release to Elsewhere. • Newchildren are sent to their assigned family units. • Jobs are assigned to young people (graduates) according to their character traits. Purpose of assigning jobs: to help young people to fit in i.e. as birthmother, instructor, drone pilot, recreation leader, caretaker of the old, nurturer.	• Jonas is selected because he is intelligent, brave ... • He has the "capacity to see beyond". • Jonas' training involves pain. • He is brave enough to be selected as the next Receiver of Memory.

3.3 Lesson 3: What does "love" mean?

Goals:

- **Content:** Students get to know that love is forbidden in the Community.
- **Language:** Watching to extract relevant information; reflecting and speaking about the absence of love and the absence of language to describe feelings.

Material:

Film scene about Jonas' dream and love (41–45);

Worksheets 1–2, pp. 77–78

Activities

Step 1: Students watch the scene that runs from 0:41:00 – 0:45:00 several times. They fill in the gaps in the screenplay (Worksheet 1). One pair gets the Worksheet as a transparency.

Step 2: Worksheets are compared and questions about love (family love and sexual love) are discussed in class.

Step 3: Questions about strange language and the importance of the scenes are discussed.

Expected solution to Worksheet 1:

Scene 1: *Jonas watches Fiona brushing her hair in the opposite house.*

LOUDSPEAKER: Citizens are reminded that sleep period commences in 15 minutes. Thank you.

Jonas dreams of himself and Fiona as a couple at a wedding dance. They kiss and are happy.

Scene 2: *Jonas and the Giver are talking while taking a walk.*

JONAS: It was like a memory, **but Fiona was there.**

GIVER: You had a **dream**.

JONAS: A what?

GIVER: A **dream**. A combination of **reality, fantasy, emotions** and what you had for dinner.

Jonas and the Giver both smile.

GIVER: You have stopped taking your injections, haven't you?

JONAS: **The emotion was so strong.** And at the wedding, everybody all together laughing and dancing. The old with the young. The bride and the groom. There was something there. But different to what we have.

GIVER: Yes. We don't have that any more.

JONAS: What do you mean by that?

GIVER: I'm talking about what you feel for someone else. The mind can't explain it and you can't make it go away.

JONAS: What is it?

GIVER: **Love.** It's called "**love**".

JONAS: **Love.**

Scene 3: *Jonas and Fiona meet in the street riding their bikes. They smile at each other.*

FIONA: Oh, hi.

JONAS: Hi.

FIONA: So, what's new?

JONAS: What's new with you?

FIONA: Whatever is new?

Jonas stares at Fiona.

FIONA: Why are you being weird?

JONAS: I'm not.

Fiona looks at him, embarrassed.

JONAS: I'm just. I'm just ... *(rides off)*

Scene 4: *Father and Lily are playing with Gabriel. Jonas joins them.*

FATHER: Hold on to the hippo, Gabe. Hold on.

JONAS: Do you **love** me?

MOTHER: Jonas, precision of **language**, please!

LILY: What does "love" mean?

FATHER: I got him.

MOTHER: Jonas used a word that is so antiquated that it no longer has any application.

FATHER: If you ask: "Do you **enjoy** me?" The answer would certainly be "yes". Or: "Do your mother and I **take pride in** your accomplishments?" Of course we do. Do you understand?

JONAS: Yes, I finally do.

Scene 5: *Gabe is crying.*

JONAS: Hey Gabe. (*Makes sounds to cheer Gabe up.)*

Da. Boo. Boo-pa. Boo-pa. I love you, Gabriel.

Gabe makes happy sounds. Images of animals, colors, children etc.

Solution to **Questions 1–3 on Worksheet 2:**

2. Jonas understands that there is no real love; there are no real emotions in the Community. He becomes more and more thoughtful.
3. Jonas' loving care makes Gabe calm down. The pictures show animals, colorful pictures, joyful children, everything that the Community does not have.
4. The scenes show that both sexual love (Jonas' dream of kissing Fiona) and family love have been erased from the Community.

3.4 Lessons 4 and 5: The real meaning of "release" and Jonas' decision to escape to Elsewhere

Goals:
- **Content:** Students understand that Jonas has to escape in order to save Gabriel.
- **Language:** Viewing and listening comprehension; using new words in context.

Material:

Film scene: Jonas' father "releases" a twin (0:52:15 – 1:00:00)

Worksheet 3, p. 79

Activities

Step 1: Teacher reads and (if necessary) explains jumbled statements.

Step 2: Student pairs put the strips into chronological order.

Step 3: Students watch the film excerpt (0:52:15 – 1:00:00) and check if their order is correct.

Step 4: Reasons for Jonas' escape are discussed in class.

Solution to Worksheet 3:

1. Jonas sees his father releasing a twin. He is devastated *(außer sich)*.
2. Jonas sees children playing and wants to give up being the receiver. He wants his childhood back.
3. Jonas meets Fiona at the waterfall and asks her about her feelings; she is confused and scared when Jonas kisses her. He asks her to stop taking the daily injections.
4. Jonas remembers his first dream of the "stirrings", after which he had to take medicine regularly.
5. At his house, Jonas learns about Gabe's impending *(drohend)* release. Jonas finds that his theory is true: release means murder.
6. Jonas hurries out of the house; he tries to convince Asher that he is on an important mission. When Asher tries to stop him, Jonas knocks him down.
7. At the Giver's house, Jonas tells him that he wants to leave; the Giver supports him.

Task: *Write one sentence about the reason why Jonas thinks he has to leave.*
Possible solution: Jonas has to leave because he has seen that Gabe is in danger.

3.5 Lesson 6 and 7: The Giver and the Chief Elder argue about the Community

Material:

Film scene in which the Giver and the Chief Elder discuss the Community (1:17:47 – 1:20:14)

Worksheet 4, p. 80

Goals:

- **Content:** Students reflect on and discuss the reason why the Community decided to bring about "sameness" in the new society.
- **Language:** Viewing and listening comprehension; matching characters and statements; writing and discussing (in roles) the pros and cons (repetition of vocabulary in context)

Activities:

Step 1: The teacher tells students what happened in the scenes prior to the one they are going to watch (see scene sequence, pp. 58–63); students should know about Asher's finding and "losing" Jonas, and the impending release of Fiona and the Giver.

Step 2: Statements of characters are read aloud. Possible questions are clarified.

Step 3: Students watch the scene in which Fiona is about to be released and the Giver discusses the new society at a tribunal before the Elders' Committee. (1:17:47–1:20:14) The Chief Elder reminds the Giver why they had decided to eliminate memories.

Step 4: Students match characters with sentences and find the correct sequence (Worksheet).

Step 5: Distribute role cards containing the names/roles: Asher, Fiona, Jonas, the Giver, Jonas' mother, Jonas' father, the Chief Elder. Students assigned the same role form groups and write down their arguments for or against the new society from their role's perspective. Arguments from previous scenes should be incorporated: for example, what students found out about language, families, birthmothers, climate control, sameness etc.

Role card example:

> **Elder**
> **Pros:**
> We have a good life. We do not have to fear wars, starvation or sunburn. We are safe.
> We don't have to worry about managing our lives. Everything is taken care of. Food is delivered, houses are provided, spouses are chosen. We have birthmothers who give birth for us … We live a carefree life.

Step 6: **Panel discussion:** Eight people (one from each character group) are on the panel. The rest of the class jumps in when the panelist runs out of arguments. The teacher is the host (mediator). At the end a class vote for or against the new society is cast.

Solution to Worksheet 4:

Sequence	Speaker	Quote
11	The Giver	Do you know what it's like? To love some-one? I do.
1	The Giver	You can stop this.
2	Chief Elder	If you don't want to see it, […] close your eyes.
4	Jonas' father	Are you all comfortable?
16	Chief Elder	You know what it feels like when men blow each other up.
10	The Giver	I could not be more precise.
19	Chief Elder	Love is just a passion that can turn.
5	Fiona	I am not uncomfortable, I'm afraid.
9	Chief Elder	Precision of language.
12	The Giver	I've cried, I've sung, danced.
13	The Giver	I felt real joy.
21	Chief Elder	People are weak.
8	The Giver	I loved her.
6	Jonas' father	You know me.
14	Chief Elder	You should know better than anyone.
3	Loudspeaker	Ceremony of release to Elsewhere.
22	Chief Elder	People are selfish.
20	The Giver	We could choose better.
15	Chief Elder	You have seen children starve.
7	Jonas' father	I'll be very gentle, I promise.
23	Chief Elder	When people have the freedom to choose, they choose wrong, every single time.
18	The Giver	With love comes fate, comes hope.
17	Chief Elder	You and Jonas want to open that door again and bring all that back.

Correct sequence:

Sequence	Speaker	Quote
1	The Giver	You can stop this.
2	Chief Elder	If you don't want to see it, […] close your eyes.
3	Loudspeaker	Ceremony of release to Elsewhere.

4	Jonas' father	Are you all comfortable?
5	Fiona	I am not uncomfortable, I'm afraid.
6	Jonas' father	You know me.
7	Jonas' father	I'll be very gentle, I promise.
8	The Giver	I loved her.
9	Chief Elder	Precision of language.
10	The Giver	I could not be more precise.
11	The Giver	Do you know what it's like? To love some-one? I do.
12	The Giver	I've cried, I've sung, danced.
13	The Giver	I felt real joy.
14	Chief Elder	You should know better than anyone.
15	Chief Elder	You have seen children starve.
16	Chief Elder	You know what it feels like when men blow each other up.
17	Chief Elder	You and Jonas want to open that door again and bring all that back.
18	The Giver	With love comes fate, comes hope.
19	Chief Elder	Love is just a passion that can turn.
20	The Giver	We could choose better.
21	Chief Elder	People are weak.
22	Chief Elder	People are selfish.
23	Chief Elder	When people have the freedom to choose, they choose wrong, every single time.

3.6 Lesson 8: The ending

Material:

Film scene: Jonas finds the home (1:20:14 – end)

Worksheet 5, p. 81

Goals:

- **Content:** Understanding and critical discussion of the ending
- **Language:** Viewing, listening, note taking, discussing

Step 1: The ending is watched (from 1:20:15).

Step 2: Students take notes while watching the ending for the second time.

Step 3: The ending is either discussed in class or students each write a review focusing on the last scene.

Expected outcome:

Population	The population is observed with cameras at all times.
The Giver's help	The Giver transmits last memories to Jonas. He gives him strength and says that he loves him.
Prosecution of "the rebel"	Jonas kidnaps Gabe. Jonas' mother helps the Chief Elder to pursue him. "Jonas is a rebel."
Fiona's and Jonas' trick	Fiona helps Jonas to confuse the police so that they follow her instead of him. Fiona says she does not want to leave with him.
Asher and Jonas	Jonas steals a motorbike. He is initially pursued by the police and later by Asher in a drone.
The search	Jonas jumps from the edge. The loudspeaker announces that the search is terminated.
Jonas beyond the edge	Jonas goes through the desert thinking about his mission.
The Chief Elder, Asher and the Giver	Asher and the Giver are questioned by the Chief Elder. They are going to continue the search. The Giver and Fiona are arrested. The Chief Elder asks Asher to find him and then "lose" him.
Fiona in prison	Fiona is to be released. She tells Jonas' mother that she had felt things that have been stolen from her and everybody else. Before being released, Fiona uses the word "afraid" instead of "uncomfortable".
The ending	Jonas finds the sled to go down to the house, where a Christmas carol is being sung. The Giver addresses Jonas' mother as a mother, who should feel loss, pain, love, like her son. He says they are living a life of shadows (1:22:00). The memories return to the Community.

3.7 Lesson 9: A test

This is a suggestion for a test. Depending on the class level, teachers have to decide if they want to have their learners do all the tasks, or only a few or even change them. For example, for weak verb forms and tenses can be changed according to the subjects and the context so that only comprehension is tested, but no grammar.

If teachers want to do every task, they should allow for two lessons.

Task 2 could also be completed as an oral exam.

Material:

Worksheet 6.1–6.3, pp. 82–84

Expected solutions:

1. Summary

The film *The Giver* is about Jonas, who has to **escape** his well-protected utopian **Community** in order to **save** Gabriel, a baby who has not developed as well as other babies. He **cries** a lot and can only be calmed down by Jonas and his friend Fiona.

Both teenagers and their friend Asher are **nervous** before the ceremony because that is when they will be **assigned** jobs. Fiona gets the position of nurturer; that means she takes care of babies in the **nurturing** center. Asher will be **trained** as a drone pilot. But Jonas gets the most important position in the Community: he is selected to be the new **Receiver** of memory by the former Receiver, who thus becomes the Giver.
During his training Jonas gets transmitted all the **memories** of the past, of good and bad things, that the Community has **gotten rid of**. The Community wants **sameness**, no differences. That means weather, colors, joy, music, dance, feelings, and above all love do not exist. Neither does war exist. Babies are artificially produced, and **birthmothers,** a job that has a bad reputation, give birth. The Community chooses spouses and assigns **children** to them, who make up a "family unit". Differences are not allowed. Everybody has to **fit in**.
When Jonas learns that the word **"release"** means murder and that Gabe will be killed because he is **different** from other babies, he **kidnaps** him and escapes. The Chief Elder has Asher **pursue** him. Asher catches and loses him again so that Jonas can reach **Elsewhere**, a world that is similar to our world. Since Fiona helped Jonas to **kidnap** the baby, she is to be "released". At the end, shortly before Jonas' father can **kill** her, Jonas reaches Elsewhere and the memories **return** to the Community. Thus he is able to **save** Fiona

2. Characterizations:

	a) Characters' statements	**b) Characterization (job, experiences and character traits; outward appearance)**
The Giver	*I could not be more precise.* *I've cried, I've sung, danced.* *I felt real joy.* *I love you, Jonas.* *We could choose better.* *With love comes fate, comes hope.* *Our people created sameness.*	• former receiver of memory, transmits old memories on to Jonas • wise: knows the past and the present • helps Jonas to become a moral human being • helps him to decide to save Gabriel, Fiona, to bring back memories • helps Jonas to have compassion, pity • has known real joy • loved Rosemary and loves Jonas • thinks that love is a deep emotion every-body should have • old man
Chief Elder	*Love is just a passion that can turn.* *People are weak.* *People are selfish.* *When people have the freedom to choose they choose wrong, every single time.* *You and Jonas want to open that door again and bring all that back.* *I want you to find Jonas. I want you to lose him.* *All your training has been to fit in.*	• represents the Community government • wants to keep the Community as it is • wants people to fit in, to be the same • thinks that people are weak and cannot use their freedom to their advantage • asks Asher to follow Jonas, but drop him (Does she think he will die?) • rather old, straight blond hair, no make-up ... • ...
Jonas	*Do you feel anything? Does it feel warm? Does it feel nice?* *It was like a memory, but Fiona was there.*	• is trained to be the receiver of memory (see The Giver) • learns that what he experienced so far is not real

Jonas	*Fiona, there is more, so much more.* *Father, do you love me?* *Asher, if you ever were my friend, can you please trust me?* *I always felt I saw things differently.* *Who wants to be different?*	• had no deep emotions, but now experiences love: love for Gabriel, Fiona, The Giver • realizes that he has to save Gabriel and escape • brings back the memories of the past
Fiona	*I am not uncomfortable, I'm afraid.* *I'm terrified.*	• Jonas' best friend • is assigned the job as nurturer • is good with small children • learns from Jonas what love is • helps Jonas to kidnap Gabriel and is arrested • is prepared for "release" (to be killed) • is afraid of being killed
Asher	*I do trust you, Jonas.*	• Jonas' best friend • is assigned the job of drone pilot • is trusted by the Chief Elder • wants to stop Jonas from escaping • follows him in his drone, catches him and Gabriel, drops them into a river
Jonas' father	*Are you comfortable? You know me.* *I'll be very gentle, I promise.*	• is a nurturer • father of two "assigned" children • is a typical citizen of the Community • does not understand Jonas' question: "Do you love me?" • corrects the wording to: "Do you take pride …?" • brings Gabriel home so that he can grow • releases babies who are different or who are twins • is on the verge of releasing Fiona • wants to do it gently
Jonas' mother	*Jonas used a word that is so antiquated that it has no application today.* *Precision of language.*	• is a kind of judge (works in the justice department) • is a typical citizen of the Community • is strict and harsh: always reminds Jonas of proper behavior and proper language • mother of two "assigned" children

3. The Ending: novel & film

Similarities:

- They are riding on a sled downhill, rather fast.
- Jonas is hearing music that people are singing.
- They are safe.

Differences:

- The music Jonas hears is "Silent Night", a Christmas carol.
- In the book, the memories have not yet returned.
- The people in Elsewhere are waiting for them.
- In the book, the Community does not play a role anymore.

Oral exam

Come up with a discussion between The Giver and the Chief Elder
Before The Giver applies for release, the Chief Elder and The Giver have an argument about what has happened to the community after they decided on Sameness. Imagine what they might say concerning the original intention and actual results.

Expected outcome
This is what they say in their discussion of the new society (The Community) before Fionas's impending release:

The Giver	The Chief Elder
Sameness seemed good at the beginning: we could get rid of differences among people	*We wanted sameness to make sure that everybody fitted into society. We had to decide for the people because people are weak and selfish. When people have the freedom to choose they choose wrong, every single time. You and Jonas want to open that door again and bring all the bad things back.*
But then I realized: Sameness also means no individuality, no real feelings, no joy, no love. With love comes fate, comes hope.	*Love is just a passion that can turn.*

4. Worksheets

You will watch a sequence of five short scenes (41:00–45:00) several times.

1. *After watching it once in order to understand the content, watch it again and fill in the gaps in the screenplay below. Compare your results with a partner.*

Scene 1: *Jonas watches Fiona brushing her hair in the opposite house.*

LOUDSPEAKER: Citizens are reminded ______________________________.

Jonas dreams of himself and Fiona being a couple at a wedding dance. They kiss and are happy.

Scene 2: *Jonas and the Giver are talking while taking a walk.*

JONAS: It was like a memory, ______________________________.

GIVER: You had a ____________.

JONAS: A what?

GIVER: A ____________. A combination of ______________________ and what you had for dinner.

Jonas and the Giver both smile.

GIVER: You have stopped taking your injections, haven't you?

JONAS: ______________________. And at the wedding, everybody all together laughing and dancing. The old with the young. The bride and the groom. There was something there. But different to what we have.

GIVER: Yes. We don't have that any more.

JONAS: What do you mean by that?

GIVER: I'm talking about what you feel for someone else. The mind can't explain it and you can't make it go away.

JONAS: What is it?

GIVER: ______________________. It's called ______________________.

JONAS: ______________________.

Scene 3: *Jonas and Fiona meet in the street riding their bikes. They smile at each other and have a short chat.*

Scene 4: *Father and Lily are playing with Gabriel. Jonas joins them.*

FATHER: Hold on to the hippo, Gabe. Hold on.

JONAS: Do you ______________________ me?

MOTHER: Jonas, precision of ______________________. Please?!

LILY: What does "love" mean?

FATHER: I got him.

MOTHER: Jonas used a word that is so antiquated that it no longer has any application.

FATHER: If you ask: "Do you ______________________ me?" The answer would certainly be "yes". Or: "Do your mother and I ______________________ your accomplishments?" Of course we do. Do you understand?

JONAS: Yes, I finally do.

Scene 5: *Gabe is crying. Jonas soothes him until he make happy sounds.*

ISBN 978-3-12-578137-5

1. With a partner write a few notes about Jonas' statement:
"I finally do (understand)."
What does he understand?

2a. What does Jonas do to calm Gabe down?

2b. At the end of the scene there are different pictures that Jonas and Gabe both see. What are they and what do they stand for?

3. Discuss with your partner:
Why do you think these scenes are very important in the whole film? What does the sequence reveal about the Community? What do you think might happen next?

ISBN 978-3-12-578137-5

The real meaning of 'release' and Jonas' decision of escape

1. *Cut out the statements below and put them into the right order. Discuss your results in class.*
2. *After you have decided on the right order for the statements, write one sentence about the reason why Jonas thinks he has to leave:*

- -

At his house, Jonas learns about Gabe's impending *(drohend)* release. Jonas finds that his theory is true: release means murder.

- -

At the Giver's house, Jonas tells him that he wants to leave; the Giver supports him.

- -

Jonas hurries out of the house; he tries to convince Asher that he is on an important mission. When Asher tries to stop him, Jonas knocks him down.

- -

Jonas meets Fiona at the waterfall and asks her about her feelings; she is confused and scared when Jonas kisses her. He asks her to stop taking the daily injections.

- -

Jonas remembers his first dream of the "stirrings", after which he had to take medicine regularly.

- -

Jonas sees children playing and wants to give up being the receiver. He wants his childhood back.

- -

Jonas sees his father releasing a twin. He is devastated *(außer sich)*.

- -

ISBN 978-3-12-578137-5

The Giver and the Chief Elder argue about the Community

Who says what and when?

1. Write the names (Chief Elder, Fiona, Jonas' father, The Giver, Loudspeaker) of the people who say each sentence in the middle column.

2. Then decide on the correct sequence. In which order are these statements made?

Sequence	Speaker	Quote
		Do you know what it's like? To love someone? I do.
		You can stop this.
		If you don't want to see it, [...] close your eyes.
		Are you all comfortable?
		You know what it feels like when men blow each other up.
		I could not be more precise.
		Love is just a passion that can turn.
		I am not uncomfortable, I'm afraid.
		Precision of language.
		I've cried, I've sung, danced.
		I felt real joy.
		People are weak.
		I loved her.
		You know me.
		You should know better than anyone.
		Ceremony of release to Elsewhere.
		People are selfish.
		We could choose better.
		You have seen children starve.
		I'll be very gentle, I promise.
		When people have the freedom to choose, they choose wrong, every single time.
		With love comes fate, comes hope.
		You and Jonas want to open that door again and bring all that back.

ISBN 978-3-12-578137-5

The Ending

Watch the ending of the film twice and take notes when watching it for the second time. What do you find out about the points below? Complete the table.

Population	
The Giver's help	
Prosecution of "the rebel"	
Fiona's and Jonas' trick	
Asher	
The search	
Jonas beyond the edge	
The Chief Elder	
Fiona in prison	
The ending	

ISBN 978-3-12-578137-5

Name: ____________________

Task 1: *Complete the summary with some of these words. Not all words fit. Be careful: some of the words have to be changed (nouns in singular or plural, verb form in the right tense ...). You can also use other words if they match the content.*

assign, birthmother, children, Community, cry, different, Elsewhere, emotions/feelings, erase (eliminate), escape, fit in, job/position, kidnap, kill, leave, love, memory, nervous (scared), nurturing, pursue, Receiver, release, return, sameness, save (2), train

Summary

The film The Giver is about Jonas, who has to ____________ his well-protected utopian ____________ in order to ____________ Gabriel, a baby who has not developed as well as other babies. He cries a lot and can only be calmed down by Jonas and his friend Fiona.

Both teenagers and their friend Asher are ____________ before the ceremony because that is when they will be ____________ jobs. Fiona gets the ____________ of nurturer; that means she takes care of babies in the ____________ center. Asher will be ____________ as a drone pilot. But Jonas gets the most important position in the Community: he is selected to be the new ____________ of memory by the former receiver, who thus becomes the Giver.

During his training Jonas gets transmitted all the ____________ of the past, of good and bad things, that the Community has ____________. The Community wants ____________, no differences. That means weather, colors, joy, music, dance, feelings, and above all ____________ do not exist. Neither does war exist. Babies are artificially produced, and ____________, a job that has a bad reputation, give birth. The Community chooses spouses and assigns ____________ to them, who make up a "family unit". Differences are not allowed. Everybody has to ____________.

When Jonas learns that the word "____________" means murder and that Gabe will be killed because he is ____________ from other babies, he ____________ him and escapes. The Chief Elder has Asher ____________ him. Asher catches and loses him again so that Jonas can reach ____________, a world that is similar to our world.

Since Fiona helped Jonas to ____________ the baby, she is to be "released". At the end, shortly before Jonas' father can ____________ her, Jonas reaches Elsewhere and the memories return to the Community. Thus he is able to ____________ Fiona.

ISBN 978-3-12-578137-5

Name: ____________________

Task 2:

2a: *Match the statements below to the characters: The Giver, Chief Elder, Jonas, Fiona, Asher, Jonas' father, Jonas' mother, by referring to their statements below. Then complete 2b.*

Character:	**Statements/Quotes:**
	Are you comfortable? You know me.
	It was like a memory, but Fiona was there.
	I could not be more precise.
	Love is just a passion that can turn.
	Do you feel anything? Does it feel warm? Does it feel nice?
	Fiona, there is more, so much more.
	Father, do you love me.
	Jonas is using a word that is so antiquated that it no longer has any application.
	I am not uncomfortable, I'm afraid.
	Precision of language.
	I've cried, I've sung, danced.
	I'm terrified.
	I felt real joy.
	People are weak.
	I love you, Jonas.
	People are selfish.
	We could choose better.
	I'll be very gentle, I promise.
	When people have the freedom to choose they choose wrong, every single time.
	With love comes fate, comes hope.
	You and Jonas want to open that door again and bring all that back.
	I want you to find Jonas. I want you to lose him.
	Asher, if you ever were my friend, can you please trust me?
	I do trust you, Jonas.
	I always felt I saw things differently. Who wants to be different?
	Our people created sameness.
	All your training has been to fit in.

2b: *Choose one character and write about his/her job, experiences and character traits. You may also write about his/her outward appearance.*

ISBN 978-3-12-578137-5

Name: ____________________

Task 3: The ending

Read this short extract of the novel *The Giver*. Then answer the question below the excerpt.

The novel's last two paragraphs:

Downward, downward, faster and faster. Suddenly he was aware with certainty and joy that below, ahead, they were waiting for him; and that they were waiting, too, for the baby. For the first time, he heard something that he knew to be music. He heard people singing.

Behind him, across vast distances of space and time, from the place he had left, he heard music too. But perhaps it was only an echo.

Lois Lowry, *The Giver*, Ernst Klett Sprachen, Stuttgart 1998, p. 136, ll. 19–25

To what extent is the ending of the film similar to and different from the novel's ending?

ISBN 978-3-12-578137-5

IV Additional Materials

The following materials provide background information. You might want to read them yourself, but you may also distribute them in class for further discussion. This section contains a number of **reviews**, which you might want to use as examples for your students. There are also two **interviews** with Louis Lowry (one long before the film was made in 1998 and a recent one from 2015, after the film was released.

Overview of Copymasters:

Copymaster A, p. 86: What other people think about *The Giver*

Copymaster B, p. 87: What the author says about *The Giver*

Copymaster C, pp. 88–89: Interview with Lois Lowry in September 1998

Copymaster D, pp. 90–91: E-mail interview with Lois Lowry from February 2015

What other people think about *The Giver*

1 Stephen R. Perrault

The Giver is very reminiscent of Huxley's *Brave New World* and Orwell's *Nineteen Eighty-Four*. As in *Brave New World*, children are born outside of a family unit and spend time being raised by the society. As in *1984*, there are speakers in every room and members of the society are heard and addressed. In many ways, *The Giver* is a new wine in an old bottle.
The greatest difference between *The Giver* and the previous works of Utopian fiction is that the reader is treated to a young adult protagonist. Jonas is in many ways typical of an average eleven- or twelve-year-old. He enjoys sports, becomes annoyed with his little sister, and has a best friend. This makes for an excellent tour guide as students will easily relate to Jonas as a protagonist. Students will also respond to Lowry's sense of suspense. Throughout the novel, Lowry pulls the reader through various hoops of anticipation, culminating in the Nurturing Center's decision to release Gabriel. By making the familiar unfamiliar, Lowry is able to spring surprise after surprise on a reader who is never sure what is secure between their world and the one of Jonas' Community.
The Giver would be a wonderful book to include in a unit on conformity and nonconformity. It would also be a nice literary connection to a history lesson on communism and the Soviet Union. I could also see using this novel in a religion class, making comparisons between the Receiver of Memory and Christ (only in Catholic School). *The Giver* would also serve as a nice companion to the *Chocolate War, 1984, Brave New World*, or *Animal Farm*.

Stephen R. Perrault in *What to Read. An Adolescent Literature Web Site* (maintained by Jane Butler) about *The Giver*

2 Kirkus Review

In a radical departure from her realistic fiction and comic chronicles of Anastasia, Lowry creates a chilling, tightly controlled future society where all controversy, pain, and choice have been expunged, each childhood year has its privileges and responsibilities, and family members are selected for compatibility. As Jonas approaches the "Ceremony of Twelve" he wonders what his adult "Assignment" will be. Father, a "Nurturer", cares for "newchildren"; Mother works in the "Department of Justice"; but Jonas' admitted talents suggest no particular calling. In the event, he is named "Receiver", to replace an Elder with a unique function: holding the Community's memories – painful, troubling, or prone to lead (like love) to disorder; the Elder ("The Giver") now begins to transfer these memories to Jonas. The process is deeply disturbing; for the first time Jonas learns about ordinary things like color, the sun, snow, and mountains, as well as love, war, and death: the ceremony known as "release" is revealed to be murder. Horrified, Jonas plots to escape to "Elsewhere", a step he believes will return the memories to all the people, but his timing is upset by a decision to release a newchild he has come to love. Ill-equipped, Jonas sets out with the baby on a desperate journey whose enigmatic conclusion resonates with allegory: Jonas may be a Christ figure, but the contrasts here with Christian symbols are also intriguing. Wrought with admirable skill – the emptiness and menace underlying this Utopia emerge step by step: a richly provocative novel. (Fiction 12+)

From: *Kirkus Reviews*, January 3, 1993. Copyright 2015 Kirkus Media LLC

ISBN 978-3-12-578137-5
Klett

What the author says about *The Giver*

1 From *Ask the Author*

My books have varied in content and style. Yet it seems to me that all of them deal, essentially, with the same general theme: the importance of human connections.

A *Summer to Die*, my first book, is a fictionalized retelling of the early death of my sister, and of the effect of such a loss on a family. *Number the Stars*, set in a different culture and era, tells of the same things: the role that we humans play in the lives of our fellow beings. […] *The Giver* takes place against the background of yet another very different culture and time. Though broader in scope than my earlier books, it nonetheless speaks to the same concern: the vital needs for humans to be aware of their interdependence, not only with each other, but the world and its environment.

http://www.ipl.org/youth/Ask Author/Lowry.html

2 From the Newbery Medal acceptance speech

Every author is asked again and again the questions we probably each have come to dread the most: How did you get this idea? We give glib, quick answers because there are other hands raised, other kids in the audience waiting. I'd like, tonight, to dispense with my usual flippancy and glibness and try to tell you the origins of this book. It is a little like Jonas looking into the river and realizing that it carries with it everything that has come from an Elsewhere. A spring, perhaps, at the beginning, bubbling up from the earth; then a trickle from a glacier; a mountain stream entering farther along; and each tributary bringing with it the collected bits and pieces from the past, from the distant, from the countless Elsewheres: all of it moving, mingled, in the current. For me, the tributaries are memories, and I've selected only a few. I'll tell them to you chronologically. I have to go way back. I'm starting forty-six years ago.

The Horn Book Magazine 94, p. 414–426

ISBN 978-3-12-578137-5

Interview with Lois Lowry, Sept. 1998

The following interview took place on September 10, 1998 in Margret Lowry's home in Roehl/Bitburg by Mechthild Hesse and Hartmut K. Selke.

Q: Why did you choose the title "The Giver"?
LL: I never write a title until after I've written the book. Some authors write a title and then write the book, but I never know what a book is about until after I've finished it.
I considered various titles and *The Receiver* was one of them. I don't remember exactly why I chose *The Giver.* I always tell the kids that the best title of any book ever written was *Jaws*. Nobody ever forgets that title. And *The Giver* is a similarly easy title which says something about the book without giving too much away.
If, for example, I had called it, as they apparently did in Germany, *The Guardian of Memory*, it would be too much, I think. It's better to keep it very concise.

Q: Does this also mean that the Giver in the book is more central than we think he is?
LL: Well, if you try to identify the protagonist, or the main character, I think it would be the boy. But the Giver is more central, and has more depth; and that's why, I guess, I put the picture on the cover of the man, rather than the boy. Without the man – and his memories – the boy would be powerless.

Q: I had the impression he was quite a subversive character, actually, which I found surprising.
LL: Subversive? In what sense?

Q: Well, he readily agrees with Jonas that something is wrong in that society, that the two of them – that was the initial plan – should change it. He becomes increasingly cynical at the end, don't you think?
LL: I should have re-read the book before I came; it's been a while. But, perhaps, that's because he has not before had a colleague until this boy appears. He's spent a long time alone and so, perhaps, that's why he grasps at the relationship with the boy to enhance what's always been in him. You know, the desire to change things.
I think he's an unhappy character.

Q: I just mentioned the Internet. When you type in Lois Lowry – Giver do you know how many hits you get?
LL: Thousands! I've gone through and occasionally opened one up. A lot of them, I find, are children's book reports.

Q: Well, I find this utterly amazing, that kids feel the urge to write about this book on the Internet. But you have other things as well: You have college reading lists, you have teaching notes. Have you got an explanation for this incredible success?

ISBN 978-3-12-578137-5

LL: It's astonishing to me, I don't know if you're aware of this: *The Giver* was published in the U.S. in 1993; and it is still number one on the bestseller list (for children's books) in *Publishers Weekly*, after 5 years. If a writer sits down and thinks, yeah, I'd like to write a book now that will be on the bestseller list for years and years and years, and will cause a lot of controversy, and be read all over the world, you could never think of a book that would do that. I certainly didn't sit down to do that. It's not something you can plan. And that that has happened has been amazing. I'm not certain why it has happened. I'm sure if you've looked through all those hits on the Internet, you'll discover also that some of them, fortunately few, are conservative, fundamentalist groups who want to have the book removed from the schools. It's very controversial in the United States. It's on the list of the 10 most challenged books in the United States. There have been public meetings and hearings, all about this book, which seemed, when I wrote it, to be not a controversial book. It seemed to be just kind of a good story. But it has taken on more than that, and there are churches and religious groups that use it in a positive way as well as other religious groups that find it objectionable. It's even used in prisons as prisoners' reading. So it has just found all these avenues beyond the average child audience that I've always written for and to, and how that has happened, I don't know. It's not something that you could cause to happen. It's something that has arisen out of the material that has struck a lot of chords in people, politically. It's considered a very political book, it's considered a religious book. It just has all these different elements to it that I was not aware of putting into it. I can see that they're there, but I didn't consciously put them there.

Q: The Giver is very different from the other books that you have written. The future is something that always fascinates my students, my 15- to 16-year-olds, and that's why I think it will be a success in the classroom, too, because they have all these ideas about the future, and they can then discuss them.
LL: In our country, two particular futuristic books – Orwell, *1984*, and Huxley, *Brave New World* – have always been required reading in high school or, later, in college. So we in the U.S. all grow up familiar with those, and many reviewers compared *The Giver* to those.

Q: What about you, do you think you were influenced by them?
LL: I think everybody is influenced by everything they read, and I have read Huxley and Orwell when I was a student, and more recently I've read Margaret Atwood, *The Handmaid's Tale*, which I liked a lot. Incidentally, that was completely different from anything she'd written, too. I'd love to ask her where that came from. Anyway, I think I was influenced by those, but I wasn't thinking of them when I sat down to write *The Giver.* I think I was more influenced at that time with the fact that my parents were both very old and were both clearly not going to live much longer, and my father's memory had gone. But my mother, though she was very sick and also blind, still had her mental capacity quite intact, and in the last months of her life she wanted to tell me all about her childhood, and all about her entire 86 years of life. That's the only thing she wanted to do the last few months she was alive: to tell somebody those stories. They were not particularly important stories, but, clearly, she didn't want them to just disappear when she died. I think I was very aware of that when I sat down during those months – when she was still alive in fact – to write a new book. Memory was the topic that was on my mind. [...]

ISBN 978-3-12-578137-5

Q: You mentioned some time ago that you weren't sure that you would like the film that may get made of "The Giver". *Where do you see problems of turning this book into a film?*

LL: Well, the problem that they faced was that so much of the book takes place within the mind of the boy.

They had to create action to make it visual. They also felt the need to incorporate a little romance so that the relationship between the boy and the girl becomes a little greater than it had been. I believe that there's a kiss exchanged, and stuff like that. And then they felt as if they needed to put a clearer ending on it. I have read the screenplay, and it begins with an old woman telling a story, to children I believe, and it turns out that the woman is Fiona. She's talking about what has happened and she has never seen Jonas again, he's disappeared, so it gives it a bit more of a conclusion. But I think it's doubtful that the movie will be made, because the screenplay was commissioned and written two and a half years ago. I was told that Sean Connery was interested in the role of the Giver, they were trying to raise money of course, and money is always the factor on which those decisions hinge. Then Sean Connery went off to do some other movie, and then Robin Williams was interested, but the money still wasn't there, so every time I hear from them it's all up in the air.

I'm just as glad, I think, because what happens is when a film is made from a very popular book, everybody rushes to the movie and the movie is a big success for a while, and then the movie is over and people don't go to it any more. But then nobody ever buys or reads the book again. Or kids go to the movie and they never read the book at all. So, when they hear about *The Giver*, what they think of is the movie, and they never have the experience of the book. I won't be disappointed if it isn't ever made, but I don't have any control over it.

ISBN 978-3-12-578137-5

Interview with Lois Lowry, February 2015

The following is an e-mail interview with Lois Lowry, carried out by Mechthild Hesse in February 2015.

Q: Now the film has been made. It was released on DVD in February 2015. Are you happy with it?
LL: There are things I loved about it...in particular I thought the visual effect of the memories was so much more powerful than the descriptions in the book. And there were things I didn't like.

Q: Did you really not have control over it? Or did the film people (script writer, director, actors...) ask your advice?
LL: No, I had no control. A book writer rarely does, if ever. But the director sought my advice again and again, often abut small details, and kept me informed, and invited me to the set.

Q: What do you especially like about the film?
LL: I mentioned above how much I liked the portrayal of the memories. I also loved the design of The Giver's dwelling. Those massive walls of books! And I very much liked the enlargement of the character of the Chief Elder; she became mysterious, complex, and more interesting than in the book.

Q: Is there anything you don't like about it?
LL: I was sorry...though I understood the reasons...that the kids were older than in the book. And, again, though I understood the reasons, I was sorry that a movie has to lose the introspection that a book has, in favor of visual action.

Q: You predicted a romance that the novel does not have. Does it bother you that it has become very much a Hollywood film with the love story, the bike chase, the use of modern technology etc.?
LL: Once they made the kids older, it made sense that the romance had to enter. When a boy that age begins to have feelings, of course he would be attracted to his pretty teenage friend. I thought they did a good job of keeping that element relatively subdued.

Q: The protagonists are much older than your original twelve-year-olds. Does that bother you?
LL: It did at first. But when I saw the first filmed scenes, I realized that because of their environment, the 17-year-old kids were as unsophisticated and naïve as 12-year-olds. Then it seemed okay.

Q: You mention in your blog that you met with Jeff Bridges later to promote reading. Is he a big literature fan?
LL: He reads, and appreciates literature.

ISBN 978-3-12-578137-5

Q: I read that Jeff Bridges and the other adults involved in the film making read and liked the book before they started to think about it as a film. Did the book become known to so many adults because it is required reading in American middle schools?
LL: Jeff came across it because it had won the Newbery Medal, because his daughters were reading it in school, and he was looking for a book to make into a film which could star his father. I think the book is known to adults because of its popularity in schools and among kids, and because it has incited occasional controversy over the years.

Q: Do you think that now as the film is out children won't read your book anymore, as you predicted in the interview 16 years ago?
LL: That seems not to be the case. The book is still being used in schools, and the film doesn't seem to have affected its popularity.

Q: How did you get along with all the movie stars?
LL: They could not have been more pleasant to me. I liked all of them very much.

Q: Originally you left the ending open, but the film closes it. It is clear that Jonas and Gabriel have arrived where people are celebrating Christmas. Do you feel that ending is a bit on the kitsch side?
LL: I argued [about] the ending with the producer. I would have preferred to leave it as it was. But I lost that battle.

Q: When I read the book I had a very archaic society in mind. But in the film it is more futuristic. Does this agree with the Community in your imagination? The houses are very big, luxurious. The architecture is modern. Concrete has been used a lot. The landscape, too, is beautiful, welcoming once Jonas sees it in color. I expected everything to be cold, drab. What kind of environment did you have in mind?
LL: I saw it much as it was in the film, though perhaps less attractive. I grew up on military bases and I saw that kind of rigid, orderly setting in my mind when I was writing the book. But the book is, of course, set in the future; and it made sense that the architecture would be quite modern.
The landscape, filmed in South Africa, is vast and beautiful. I envisioned it less so, more like the landscape that is familiar to me. But I loved that part of the film, and the extensive, forbidding beauty.

Q: Does the triangle have a symbolic meaning?
LL: Beats me! That was a device on the part of the screenwriter and I still don't really understand it.

ISBN 978-3-12-578137-5
Klett

V Further Reading

1. *The Giver* Quartet by Lois Lowry

Since the publication of *The Giver* in 1993, Lois Lowry has written three "companions" to *The Giver*: *Gathering Blue (2000)*, *Messenger* (2004) and *Son (2014)*. She called them "companions", since they are not sequels, something that the readers wanted, especially since they were not satisfied with the open end of *The Giver*. Now the four novels are called *The Giver Quartet*.

Below there is a summary of each of the three companions and a Copymaster (E, p. 96) with an excerpt from *Son* with two writing/discussion tasks. These could be handed out to students in preparation for an oral exam or as an alternative exam, or of course as homework.

Suggested answers to tasks:

1. *Describe the procedure of how girls become birthmothers and give birth.*

- are selected at 12
- have less demanding school subjects; health and nutrition courses required
- live in special dormitories
- get good food and additional vitamins
- have to exercise and lead a healthy life
- have to undergo physical tests to be called "ready" for insemination (procedure quick and painless)
- have to be tested again and become "certified Vessels"
- blindfolded, they give birth nine months later
- have real pain

2. *Analyze a birthmother's living conditions, her role and social standing in the Community.*

- selected females
- are not smart
- must give up academically demanding subjects
- are separated from their family units at an early age
- live almost at the edge of the Community
- although necessary, have a low reputation; lowest social standing
- as "birthing machines" they are pampered with good food and vitamins
- are called "vessels", which shows that they are almost less than human
- get no information about the insemination process, pregnancy and birth (birth masks blindfold them)

Gathering Blue (2000)

The story is set in another strange, future society that is supervised by a committee of Guardians. This Community lets people with deformations die in the fields. The protagonist Kira is physically disabled (she has a deformed leg), but she has a special gift: she is a master of embroidery and weaving. That is why this pre-industrial society, based on the gifts of craftsmen and women, lets Kira live. Her task is to mend and update a beautiful robe that the Singer wears when she sings about the history of the civilization.

In the course of the book, Kira learns about the secrets of the society, for example that she and her new friends are prisoners, not allowed to leave. Then messenger Matt (the protagonist of the next novel) brings her blind father Christopher (whom she thought was dead and who is called Seer to her). He asks her to come his Village, where disabled people are allowed to live. But she wants to stay and help her own Community.

Messenger (2004)

Matt has lived in the Village with the blind Seer and is looking forward to receiving his true name, Messenger. He has discovered that he has a special gift, the gift to heal others. He is upset when he realizes that the villagers, who once were kind, gentle and friendly, are becoming cruel. They are closing their borders although they always welcomed strangers and outsiders. Leader (who is Jonas from *The Giver*) used to lead Village wisely and everybody was happy once.

When the date for closing the border is determined, Matt must make the trip through the sinister Forest that surrounds the Village to bring back the Seer's daughter Kira. On the return journey, Matt must decide if he should use his healing powers which, however, are self-destructive.

Son (2012)

Son brings all the characters from the previous novels together and finally comes up with a conclusion that readers of *The Giver* had been longing for. Whereas at the end of *The Giver* readers don't know exactly whether Jonas and Gabe live or die, it is now clear that both live.

The first part of *Son* is about Gabe's birthmother Claire who did not play a role in any of the previous novels. She had not performed well when giving birth to Gabriel and thus was sent to do a job in the fish hatchery, which did not satisfy her. To her, satisfaction would come from being a real mother. She learns this by visiting the nurturing center and observing nurturers taking care of the "newchildren". She realizes that Gabe not only responds well to Jonas' father, but also to herself. All she wants is to care for her baby. However, when a boat from Elsewhere takes off, she finds herself on that very boat.

In the second part of *Son*, Claire is washed ashore in a primitive Community, set in a valley surrounded by dangerous cliffs and rocks. There Claire sees many things for the first time, witnesses animals' and babies' births and sees and learns the names for colors. But she knows that she has to find her son. To do that, she has to go on a very dangerous journey. A mysterious figure, the Tradesman, helps her find her son. However, she has to pay a high price for finding Gabe: she has to trade her youth.

In the third and final part of *Son*, Claire – now an old woman – actually finds Gabe. He lives in a kind of boarding house for adolescents. Unaware of his mother's presence he himself yearns to find his mother and is intent on building a boat to show him the way to "the Community". Claire does not dare to talk to him, but finally talks to Jonas, who is the "Leader" of the Village. Both Jonas and Gabe still have pale blue eyes and have kept their special gifts: Jonas can still see beyond, although this gift is dwindling and Gabe has the gift of "veering", which is also something like seeing into people's souls with their innermost thoughts and feelings. With Jonas' and Gabe's gifts, they defeat Trademaster, who is the personification of evil, and thus Claire can regain her youth.

Son by Lois Lowry

Food in the Birthmothers' Dormitory was always plentiful and delicious. The Vessels were all being meticulously nourished. Of course, growing up in the Community, she had always been adequately fed. Food had been delivered to her family's dwelling each day.

But when she had been selected Birthmother at twelve, the course of life had changed. It had been gradual. The academic courses – math, science, law – at school became less demanding for her group. Fewer tests, less reading required. The teachers paid little attention to her.

Courses in nutrition and health had been added to her curriculum, and more time was spent on exercise in the outdoor air. Special vitamins had been added to her diet. Her body had been examined, tested, and prepared for her time here. After that year had passed, and part of another, she was deemed ready. She was instructed to leave her family dwelling and move to the Birthmothers' Dormitory…

There was her celebratory dinner last evening in the dwelling. Her brother, older by six years, had already gone on to his own training in the Department of Law and Justice. They saw him only at public meetings; he had become a stranger…

"Were you embarrassed when I was selected for Birthmother?" she asked them. She had, herself, secretly hoped for something more prestigious. At her brother's selection, when she had been just six, they had all been very proud. Law and justice was reserved for those of special intelligence. But she had never been a top student.

"No", her father said. "We trust the Community's judgment. They knew what you would do best."

"And Birthmother is very important," Mother added. "Without Birthmothers, none of us would be here!"

Then they wished her well in the future. Their lives were changing too; parents no longer, they would move now into the place where Childless Adults lived.

The next day, she walked alone to the dormitory attached to the Birthing Unit and moved into a small bedroom she was assigned, and the recreation field beyond. In the distance, there was a glimpse of the river that bordered the Community.

Finally, several weeks later, after she was settled in and beginning to make friends among the other girls, she was called for insemination.

Not knowing what to expect, she had been nervous. But when the procedure was complete, she felt relieved; it had been quick and painless.

"It that all?" she asked in surprise, rising from the table when the technician gestured that she should.

"That's all. Come back next week to be tested and certified."

She had laughed nervously. She wished they had explained everything more clearly in the instruction folder they had given her when she was selected. "What does 'certified' mean?" she asked.

The worker, putting away the insemination equipment, seemed a little rushed. There were probably orders waiting.

"Once they are sure it is implanted," he explained impatiently, "then you're a certified Vessel."

"Anything else?" he asked her as he turned to leave. "No? You're free to go then." […]

That all seemed such a short time ago. Now here she was, nine months later, with the blindfold strapped around her eyes. The discomfort had started some hours before, intermittently; now it was nonstop. She breathed deeply as they had instructed. It was difficult, blinded like this; her skin was hot inside the mask. She tried to relax. To breathe in and out. To ignore the discom– No, she thought. *It is pain. It really is pain.* Gathering her strength for the job, she groaned slightly, arched her back, and gave herself up to darkness. Her name was Claire. She was fourteen years old.

Tasks:

1. Describe the procedure of how girls become birthmothers and give birth.

2. Analyze a birthmother's living conditions and her role and social standing in the Community.

ISBN 978-3-12-578137-5

2. Related Literature

2.1 Other recent Young Adult dystopias

Since the turn of the millennium, there has been a boom in dystopian fiction for young people. Many of these books come in series, "spinning out extended narratives in intricately imagined worlds." Usually the books end in cliff-hangers, triggering young readers to post "half-mocking protestations of agony" in all kinds of reading forums (cf. Miller).

Due to the popularity of young adult dystopian fiction, film people try to secure filmrights directly after the novels' publication. Except for *Uglies* and *Matched*, films followed the books more or less immediately. Movies for the *Uglies* and *Matched* series are in the making.

The American writer Laura Miller considers one of the causes the nearly continuous adult supervision of teenagers. She argues that the youth-centered versions of dystopia are different from their adult predecessors in that young adult novels are less didactic. Basing her argument on the British expert Kay Sambell she says: they do not persuade readers to stop something from happening; they are about "what's happening, right this minute, in the stormy psyche of the adolescent reader". Miller refers to Scott Westerfield's blog where he says that "the success of *Uglies* is partly thanks to high school being a dystopia." American high school rules are "arbitrary, unfathomable, and subject to sudden change. A brutal social hierarchy prevails, with the rich, the good-looking, the athletic lording their advantages over everyone else. To survive you have to be totally fake ... Everyone is always watching you, scrutinizing your clothes or your friends and obsessing over whether you're having sex or taking drugs, or getting good enough grades, but no one cares who you really are or how you really feel about anything."

In contrast, Ewan Morrison thinks these dystopias are not didactic enough: He writes in *The Guardian* in September 2014 that dystopias teach children to submit to the free market, not fight authority. He criticizes books such as *The Giver, Divergent* and *Hunger Games* by saying that they are, "whether intentionally or not, substantial attacks on many of the fundamental projects and aims of the left: big government, welfare state, progress, social planning and equality. They support the idea that human nature, rather than nurture, determines how we act and live. These books propose a laissez-faire existence, with heroic individuals who are guided by innate forces of human nature against evil social planners."

Although both positions offer food for thought, for me Dan Kois' argument is the one that really does justice to Lois Lowry's work. He argues that Lowry's *The Giver Quartet* is a "corrective of sorts to *The Hunger Games* and other movie-adaptation-ready Y. A. series. Where those books feature violent death and armed rebellion, the battle that Gabriel fights in *Son* is one in which empathy and love are his only weapons. And where *The Hunger Games* features a romantic triangle among three fierce revolutionaries, *Son* highlights the undying love of a mother for her child and the child's for his mother."

(nytimes.com, 2012)

Suzanne Collins: *The Hunger Games* (2008)
The Hunger Games is probably the most popular young adult dystopian novel of the recent past. With the release of the film in 2012 it became even more popular. It is the story of 16-year-old Katniss, a brave "woman warrior", who is drafted by lottery to fight against other teenagers until only one teenager survives. The government of the North American nation Panem with its rich capital center Capitol and its 12 poor surrounding districts forces 24 combatants to fight each other. They invented the Hunger Games to distract the people from their suffering and to prevent a revolt.

The bloody fights are publicly televised and TV requirements apply: thus Katniss is exquisitely equipped and dressed by her own personal fashion maestro. She is cheered by the crowds, celebrated at galas, interviewed on national television and fed gourmet meals. She has to live a teenage girl's dream. (cf. "Fresh Hell", 2010) The rules of the competition are repeatedly changed by the authorities. When Katniss and her childhood friend Peeta, who she has fallen in love with, are the last survivors, the authorities want them to kill each other. At this point Katniss rebels. The authorities have to accept that both of them are the winners. However, since Katniss publicly defied the authorities, she becomes a target for the Capitol. She triggers a rebellion against the government, which takes place in the two sequels *Catching Fire* (2010) and *Mockingjay* (2012).

Ally Condie: *Matched* (2010)
The novel, the first of a trilogy, deals with a tightly-controlled society in which young people are "matched" with their life partners at the age of seventeen. Similar to the society in *The Giver*, there is strict population control. All citizens must carry three pills on them.

Every family has a "port" in their household that allows the government to monitor their behavior. Families are provided with dull, rationed food. Old people "die" when they are 80. The Society has eliminated most traces of culture, saving only 100 items of everything: poems, paintings, stories, songs…

Cassia Reyes is matched with her best friend Xander. When she sees this on a screen, the picture of Ky Markham, an outcast at her school, appears. Ky is an "aberration" and not supposed to be matched. (Matched people are married when they are 21.) She realizes that the young man she really loves is Ky. They read each other love poetry and writing. On his deathbed, Cassie's grandfather passes her a piece of paper with his favorite poem. However, this poem is not among the one hundred permitted poems and thus she and Ky memorize it before throwing the paper away (cf. *Fahrenheit 451*!). Her growing feelings for Ky make her question the wisdom of the Matching system. She becomes more and more frustrated with the Society's control over her relationship and her ability to express herself through poetry and writing, which is forbidden. This book is followed by *Crossed* (2011) and *Reached* (2012).

Veronica Roth: *Divergent* (2011)
In dystopian Chicago, society is divided into five factions, each dedicated to the cultivation of a particular virtue: Candor (the honest), Abnegation (the selfless), Dauntless (the brave), Amity (the peaceful), and Erudite (the intelligent). On one

day of every year, all sixteen-year-olds must select the faction to which they will devote the rest of their lives. During the highly competitive initiation process (that involves fighting others) , Beatrice renames herself Tris and struggles to determine who she is and who her friends really are. Underlying the main plot is a romantic subplot between Tris and one of her instructors in the Dauntless faction.

Dominus (2011) writes in her critique that *Divergent* and *The Hunger Games* are very similar: "Both "Divergent" and "The Hunger Games" feature appealing, but not conventionally pretty, young women with toughness to spare. Both start out with public sorting rituals that determine the characters' futures. And both put the narrators in contrived, bloody battles that are in fact competitions witnessed by an audience. Even the language sounds familiar... For a book that explores themes about the right to be individual and the importance of breaking away from the pack, *Divergent* does not exactly distinguish itself."

The trilogy consists of *Divergent* (2011), *Insurgent* (2012) and *Allegiant* (2013)

Scott Westerfield: *Uglies* (2005)
In the *Uglies'* series, all 16-year-olds undergo surgery to conform to the standard of prettiness determined by the government. Tally, the heroine of *Uglies*, looks forward to the surgery that will transform her into a Pretty and allow her to move to the party section of Pretty New Town. The Pretties are lobotomized when receiving their plastic surgery.

Only after meeting Shay and David in a Community of runaway Uglies, who show her the downsides to becoming a "Pretty", Tally rebels against society's enforced conformity. Tally learns how being a "Pretty" can change not only your look but your personality.

Tally Youngblood is looking forward to getting the pretty surgery because her best friend already lives in the pretty part of the city. But when she breaks into New Pretty Town, she meets Shay, an Ugly who is a little more rebellious. Shay and Tally argue about the pretty surgery. Shay tells Tally about a hidden town in the wilderness where no one is pretty, but Tally doesn't want to go. Unfortunately, she's been watched by Dr. Cable of the secret police (Special Circumstances), and Dr. Cable blackmails Tally into going to find this hidden town: if she doesn't help, Cable will never let Tally become a pretty. Tally is to call Cable as soon as she knows more about the hidden Community.

After some time, Tally reaches the hidden town, called the Smoke, where she's very glad to find Shay safe and sound. She also meets David, who was born in the wilderness and thus has different ideas about prettiness. He falls in love with Tally. David introduces her to his parents who tell her that the pretty surgery involves brain damage to make people manageable. Learning this, Tally decides not to call Dr. Cable and to throw her tracker in the fire. However exactly this alarms Special Circumstances who come and arrest everyone. Tally and David escape and go to the city to rescue the captives there, including David's mom and dad. But they're too late: David's dad is dead and Shay has already been turned pretty. David's mother has found a way to cure the brain damage, and Tally, feeling guilty, offers to volunteer. The first book ends with Tally confessing to David how she's responsible and giving herself up to the city authorities.

James Dashner: *The Maze Runner* (2009)
When Thomas wakes up in an elevator, he only remembers his own name, nothing else. In a completely enclosed environment (The Glade), he starts a new life along with about 60 other teenage boys who have learned to survive, on food that they grow themselves. A new boy arrives every 30 days. The original group has been in "The Glade" for two years, trying to find a way to escape through a maze that surrounds their living space. Boys are forbidden to enter the Maze and are severely punished. They have begun to give up hope, when an exhausted girl arrives with a strange note saying "She's the last one." Thomas becomes the leader of the Gladers using the information available to him and his relationships (including his ties to the girl, Teresa). The question of whether the teens will escape the maze is answered 30 pages before the book ends ...

2.2 Adult dystopias

The following pieces of literature share certain similarities with *The Giver.* Most of the titles appear in well-known anthologies and are easily available. As the list shows, *The Giver* can also fit in well with *Oberstufe* course topics such as "Visions of the Future" (Berlin), "Science and Technology" (Berlin, Sachsen, Hessen), "Individual and Society" (Bayern, Hessen, Niedersachsen, NRW), "Growing up" (Hessen).

Bradbury, Ray: *Fahrenheit 451,* various editions, first published 1953

Atwood, Margret: *The Handmaid's Tale,* New York: Fawcett Crest, 1985

Huxley, Aldous: *Brave New World.* Flamingo Modern Classics, HarperCollins (distributed in Germany by Klett Verlag, # 57766)

Le Guin, Ursula: *The Ones Who Walk Away From Omelas.* In: *The Wind's Twelve Quarters,* Harper & Row 1973. (Reprinted in many American short fiction anthologies.)

Orwell, George: *Nineteen Eighty-Four,* Penguin

Vonnegut, Kurt: "Tomorrow and Tomorrow and Tomorrow", in *Welcome to the Monkey House,* Dell

Vonnegut, Kurt: "Harrison Bergeron", in *Welcome to the Monkey House,* Dell

www.klett-sprachen.de
Online-code: hy5yx7
Or scan in the QR-code below

Excerpts from the following texts are available as Copymasters with specific tasks attached to them. You can download these from the website (www.klett-sprachen.de), using the online-code: hy5yx7.

- **George Orwell:** *The Principles of Newspeak*
- **Paul Theroux:** *The Memory Priest of the Creech People*
- **Kurt Vonnegut:** *Tomorrow and Tomorrow and Tomorrow*
- **Aldous Huxley:** *Brave New World*

VI Appendix

1. Films

1.1 Recent films based on Young Adult novels

The Giver. Director: Philip Noyce. Production Company: Walden Media. 2015. Running time: 97 Minutes
The Hunger Games. Director: Gary Ross. Production Company: Color Force, 2012 Running time: 142 Minutes
Divergent. Director: Neil Burger. Production Company: Summit Entertainment and Red Wagon Entertainment. 2014. Running time: 139 Minutes
The Maze Runner. Director: Wes Ball. Production Company: Temple Hill Entertainment. Running time: 113 Minutes

1.2 Classics based on adult dystopian novels

Nineteen Eighty-Four. Director: Michael Radford. Production Company: Virgin Films. 1984. Running time: 110 Minutes
Fahrenheit 451. Director: Francois Truffaut. Production Company: Anglo Enterprises. 1966. Running time: 112 Minutes
The Handmaid's Tale. Director: Volker Schlöndorff. Production Company: Metro-Goldwyn-Mayer. 1990. Running time: 109 Minutes
Soylent Green. Director: Richard Fleischer. Production Company: Metro-Goldwyn-Mayer. 1973. Running time: 97 Minutes

2. Bibliography

2.1 Primary literature

Collins, Suzanne: *The Hunger Games*. New York: Scholastic, *2008;* Original, but annotated: Stuttgart: Ernst Klett Sprachen, 2013
Condie, Ally: *Matched. New York:* Dutton Juvenile, 2010
Dashner, James: *The Maze Runner*. New York: Delacorte 2009
Lowry, Lois: *Gathering Blue*. Boston: Houghton Mifflin, 2000
Lowry, Lois: *Messenger*. Boston: Houghton Mifflin, 2004
Lowry, Lois: *Son*. Boston: Houghton Mifflin, 2012
Roth, Veronica: *Divergent*. New York: Katherine Tegen Books, 2011
Westerfield, Scott: *Uglies*. New York: *Simon Pulse*, 2005

2.2 Secondary literature

Dominus, Susan: "In This Utopia, Teens Must Choose Wisely". *The New York Times*, May 12, 2011 retrieved February 18 from http://www.nytimes.com/2011/05/15/books/review/young-adult-books-divergent-by-veronica-roth.html?_r=1&

Ernst, Dorothea & Kist, Heiko: *The Hunger Games. Teacher's Guide*. Stuttgart: Ernst Klett Sprachen, 2014

Field, Syd: *The Screenwriter's Workbook (revised edition).* New York: Bantam Dell, 1984.

Hesse, Mechthild: *Jugendliteratur als Sprachlehre*. Tübingen: Gunter Narr, 2001

Hesse, Mechthild: *Teenage Fiction in the Active EFL Classroom*. Stuttgart: Klett-Uniwissen 2009

Kois, Dan: "The Children's Author Who Actually Listens to Children". *New York Times*, October 3, 2012 retrieved from http://www.nytimes.com/2012/10/07/magazine/lois-lowry-the-childrens-author-who-actually-listens-to-children.html?pagewanted=all, February 18, 2015

Krück Brigitte/Loeser, Kristiane.(1997). "Effektive Rezeptionsstrategien durch Lesetagebücher". *Fremdsprachenunterricht*, 41/50 1997, 1, 2–10.

Miller, Laura (2010). "Fresh Hell. What's behind the Boom of Dystopian Fiction for Young Readers?" *The New Yorker*, June 14, 2010, retrieved February 17, 2015 from http://www.newyorker.com/magazine/2010/06/14/fresh-hell-2?currentPage=2

Morrison, Ewan: "YA dystopias teach children to submit to the free market, not to fight authority". The Guardian, September 1, 2014 retrieved from http://www.theguardian.com/books/2014/sep/01/ya-dystopias-children-free-market-hunger-games-the-giver-divergent February 18, 2015

Sambell, Kay: "Presenting the Case for Social Change." In: *Utopian and Dystopian Writing for Children and Young Adults*, p. 163–178, 2003

Wendt, Ingrid. *Starting With Little Things*, Oregon Arts Foundation, Salem, Oregon, 1983

Westerfield, Scott: http://scottwesterfeld.com/

3. Teaching magazines dealing with extensive texts

"Lesemotivation Jugendliteratur". Unterricht Englisch 89, Friedrich Verlag 2007.

In Vorbereitung: **„The Magic of Reading"**. Praxis Englisch. Westermann 3/2016.

4. URLs

Since copying out URLs is tedious and since websites and links are subject to frequent change, we have listed all the links mentioned in this Teacher's Guide on our website: www.klett-sprachen.de. Simply enter the Online-Code: 2c83qf in the search field and you will be taken directly to the page containing the links. It is there that you will find up-to-date links or information should any of the material printed here become unavailable or change sites.

www.klett-sprachen.de
Online-Code: 2c83qf
Or scan in QR-Code below:

All URLs were retrieved Febr. 19, 2015
http://www.loislowry.com/ (Lois Lowry's book, pictures, speeches … and her blog. She updates it regularly.)
http://www.npr.org/player/v2/mediaPlayer.html?action=1&t=1&islist=false&id=341283305&m=341283306 (*The Giver* film is reviewed on National Public Television, August 18, 2014)
http://www.rottentomatoes.com/m/the_giver/reviews/

The following links are meant for teachers interested in the vast field of children's literature.
Here you can find information on new books, best books, awards, secondary literature etc.
http://www.ala.org/yalsa/ (ALA: young adult literature, professional resources)
http://www.ala.org/alsc/ (American Library Association; library service to children)
http://www.dailyrecord.co.uk/whats-on/film-news/movie-review-giver-12a-97mins-4287796
http://www.dailyrecord.co.uk/by-date/19-09-2014
http://comminfo.rutgers.edu/professional-development/childlit/childrenLit (Kate Vandergrift's very useful page on Young Adult and children's literature)
http://www.irscl.com/links.html (international research library for children's literature)
http://www.nytimes.com/2012/10/07/magazine/loislowry-the-childrens-author-who-actually-listens-to-children.html?pagewanted=all)
http://www.shmoop.com/teachers/teaching-literature.html (teaching ideas, summaries of books; it is not free; you have to sign in and become a member)
http://www.goodreads.com/ (recommendations, "Best of" lists, quizzes …)